M000034445

Accountability
Citizenship

ACCOUNTABILITY
CITIZENSHIP

Thanks for being accountable!

Stephen P. Tryon

Copyright © 2013 by Stephen P. Tryon.

Library of Congress Control Number:		2013901305
ISBN:	Hardcover	978-1-4797-8356-4
	Softcover	978-1-4797-8355-7
	Ebook	978-1-4797-8357-1

All rights reserved. No part of this book may be reproduced or transmitted in any form or by any means, electronic or mechanical, including photocopying, recording, or by any information storage and retrieval system, without permission in writing from the copyright owner.

This book was printed in the United States of America.

To order additional copies of this book, contact:
Xlibris Corporation
1-888-795-4274
www.Xlibris.com
Orders@Xlibris.com

For Jake and for Pop Pop

CONTENTS

PREFACE

Accountability Citizenship began as a personal exercise in election-year therapy. Over the past 15 years or so, the level of partisanship in our political discourse, along with our apparent inability to achieve meaningful solutions to pressing issues, led me to contemplate root causes. I have concluded that the source of these problems is that not enough of us vote.

At the next level, when I considered why so few of us vote, I found something quite interesting: The decrease in voter participation stems in large measure from our failure to adapt to changes in the way our society distributes information. *Accountability Citizenship* examines this hypothesis and proposes a method for adapting to the modern information environment. The goal of adaptation is to improve the level of political participation, thereby improving the responsiveness and efficiency of our government.

I have attempted to stay on politically neutral ground throughout these pages. As most of us do, I have opinions and beliefs on specific issues, but I have tried to keep them out of this text. My reason for trying to stay neutral is simple: the prescription to cure excessive partisanship and inefficiency in a democratic republic cannot be effective if it is just another polemic from the left or the right.

That said, I owe the reader the following synopsis of my political affiliations and participation. I have been registered as a member of each major political party for periods of time spanning multiple elections. While registered as a Democrat, I voted both for Democrats and for Republicans. While registered as a Republican, I voted both for Republicans and for Democrats. I am currently registered as an Independent.

So I would characterize myself as a centrist. I have strong reactions to issues. I try to acknowledge those reactions as one point of data, evaluate the arguments proposed by people representing the two major political parties, and come to a reasoned conclusion based on what I think is best. And there, in Shakespeare's words, is the rub. What standard do I use to determine which conclusion is "best"? After all, isn't that the real root of the issue of excessive partisanship?

I think the answer to that second question is no, or at least, that the age-old debate over different conceptions of the good does not have to create partisanship and gridlock. In the tradition of Aristotle, the "good" of anything is derived from the function of that thing. The function of a clock, for instance, is to keep the time. One clock is better than another to the extent that it keeps time more accurately. So if we can agree on a function for our government, we should be able to approach a concept for good that is neutral enough for the purpose of avoiding partisan gridlock. The preamble to our Constitution offers just such a statement of purpose for our government.

Now I am not naïve enough to assume that we have universal agreement on the precise meaning of the preamble. The graceful ambiguity of those words offers room for different conceptions of the good, while at the same time affording us a common framework within which we must each derive our personal conception of the good. And that framework, inclusive of reasonable ambiguity, is the standard I apply.

The American dream is the shorthand we use to describe the opportunity that should exist in society if we are correctly applying the standards established in the Constitution. Elected officials should carry out their responsibilities in a way that advances liberty, justice and the general welfare for all Americans. Given such a framework, individuals should experience a certain quality of life. Individuals should experience the power to change their economic and social circumstances based on merit and hard work. People should be able to rise from humble roots to positions of wealth and power. I believe this American dream has been a real source of power for our country during much of our history. But many today question whether the dream is slipping away from us. In chapter five, I will examine this question in some depth. For now, and for much the same reasons I felt compelled to share a summary of my centrist roots, I offer my family's story: a story I believe exemplifies the American dream.

My grandfather on my dad's side of the family was born in upstate New York around 1895. My grandfather spent most of his childhood in foster homes. He enlisted in the army and fought in the campaign against Pancho Villa in 1916 and then in World War I. Wounded at Belleau Wood, he was discharged as a sergeant. He returned to upstate New York and married a girl he had met in one of the foster homes in which he had lived as a child. He worked the rest of his life, mostly for hourly wages and tips, raising a family of four through the Great Depression. My dad was the oldest boy. I remember my grandfather. We visited him a few times in an old house in Oneida, New York, when I was a boy.

My grandfather on my mom's side was an Irish immigrant. He enlisted to fight in WWI but was discharged before seeing combat when the war ended. I was told growing up that he received his citizenship because he had enlisted. He later owned a small grocery store in Rumson, New Jersey. As I recall the stories, he lost the store during the Depression. He also raised a family of four children during tough times. My mom was the oldest girl. I never met my mom's father. He died of cancer before I was born.

My dad enlisted in the army in 1937. He was only seventeen, so his father had to sign to allow him to join. Pop gave him thirty-five cents when he put him on the bus for the two-hundred-mile trip from Oneida to Plattsburgh, New York. My dad said it was all his father could spare at the time. In Plattsburgh, my father completed basic training in the 27th Infantry Regiment. He told me he gained twenty pounds during basic training because it was the first time in his life he remembered having three meals a day with meat every day. He became an infantryman and later acquired the specialty of radio-telephone operator.

In 1940, my dad reenlisted. He took advantage of a program that allowed reenlisting soldiers to choose advanced specialties, and chose to reenlist in the finance corps. He became a sergeant around that time and was reassigned to Fort Hancock, New Jersey. That is where he met my mom. The United States entered World War II after the Japanese attack on Pearl Harbor in December, 1941. Dad and Mom were married in September, 1942. In the fall of 1943, Dad deployed to England as part of the build-up for D-Day. My oldest brother was born in April 1944 and was two years old when my dad returned and met him for the first time.

My father landed in France as a technical sergeant on June 9, 1944. In December, while delivering a payroll to a forward unit, he was caught up in the German offensive that later became known as the Battle of the Bulge. My dad was promoted to lieutenant on the battlefield and given command of sixty stragglers. He led them through that battle, losing one to enemy action. After the battle, his promotion to the officer corps as an infantry lieutenant was formalized. He attended officer candidate school in France before joining the 94th Infantry Division for the remainder of the war. Thus without ever having had the opportunity to attend college, my father became an officer in the United States Army because of his actions in combat. He advanced through the officer ranks over a career that ultimately spanned thirty-four years, retiring as a lieutenant colonel in 1971. After his retirement, he applied his GI Bill to attend New Mexico State University and earned a master of arts in history.

My mom and dad raised eight kids, seven boys and one girl. Our sister graduated from the special education program at Mayfield High School in Las Cruces, New Mexico, in 1977 and has had a successful career spanning a number of occupations at the Saint Coletta community in Wisconsin. I am her guardian, and she spends several months each year with me or with other family members. My brothers and I all graduated from college and served in the military. Collectively, we have provided over 150 years of military service to the United States. My brother Rick continues to serve as a lieutenant general in the United States Marine Corps as of 2013.

After graduating from the United States Military Academy at West Point in 1983, I served twenty-one years in the United States Army. During my career, I served with the United Nations Command Joint Security Force (Panmunjom, Republic of Korea), the 82nd Airborne Division, and the 10th Mountain Division. In the final years of my Army career, I served as a congressional fellow to Senator Max Cleland and as a liaison to Congress for Headquarters, Department of the Army (the Pentagon). I also had the opportunity to earn a master of arts in philosophy at Stanford University (1992) in preparation for returning to West Point to teach. One of my fellow students at Stanford was Patrick Byrne, who went on to a successful business career. Byrne served as chief executive of two Berkshire Hathaway companies, Fechheimer Brothers and Centricut, before starting his own company in 1999 (Overstock.com).

As I began to contemplate life after the army, Patrick Byrne offered me a position on his executive team. I joined Overstock in August 2004, initially serving as an executive coach and project manager. I took over responsibility for the company's direct logistics operations in 2005 (fulfilling about 45 percent of the company's orders at the time). By 2007, with the help of a great team and the application of some basic leadership and management principles, we had reduced company logistics operations "per package" costs significantly. In late 2007, Patrick asked me to assume responsibility for the company's human capital management function, a role I continue in to this day.

So when I think of the American dream, I think of my dad and of all the hard work and courage... and luck... that went into his career. I think of my own experience built on the foundation my father set for me. For both my father and myself, I see a combination of hard work and luck as the main features of a tapestry spanning nearly one hundred years. This tapestry begins with my grandfather, who could only spare thirty-five cents as his son left to join the army and continues to the fantastic opportunity I enjoy today as an executive in a billion-dollar corporation. I am the American dream fulfilled.

Of course, you and I can agree that the master narrative of American dream has played a role in our nation's history while disagreeing on whether or not the dream is viable today. Likewise, those constitutional touchstones of liberty, justice and general welfare leave a great deal of room for disagreement over specific policy. The Constitution goes on, however, to prescribe mechanisms for elections whereby we choose between conflicting opinions that might exist within the general populace. These constitutional mechanisms bring me back to my initial conclusion: increasing the level of participation in our political processes is the solution to the problems of excessive partisanship and gridlock. Given adequate participation in our political process, the weight of popular opinion will determine our course and moderate the effect of special interests.

When the collective wisdom generates an outcome different from our personal convictions, we have a range of options. Depending on the moral weight we assign to the issue in question, we might choose to accept the popular verdict and move on, or we might feel compelled to continue our engagement with the political process in an effort to reverse the original choice. The choice of renouncing one's citizenship, while also an alternative, is not a practical option for most of us. Nor is this choice morally necessary, in my opinion, given the range of opportunities for peacefully expressing dissent in our society.

This brings me to another point of philosophical perspective which I should illuminate at the outset. The United States is a republic, but it is a republic in which the people exercise their sovereignty through democratically elected representatives. Some elections include referendums where citizens vote directly on specific measures—these are examples of direct democracy. In most cases, however, we vote for representatives and those representatives vote on specific legislative proposals. A classic debate in political science concerns the question of whether representatives are constrained to vote in accordance with guidance received from their constituents, or instead can vote in accordance with their judgment of what is best overall. We might call the former a more direct model, and the latter a more representative model. The issue becomes most impactful when the interests of some constituency call for support of a measure that would be harmful to the country overall, or vice versa. Some feel that the approach I prescribe in *Accountability Citizenship* is slanted toward direct democracy. I contend that people can use my model to support direct democracy, representative democracy, or a hybrid. What appears to some as a slant toward direct democracy is actually a slant toward an electorate that is fully cognizant of how its representatives are exercising their powers relative to what the people want.

Another point emerges here, and in the book as well: we don't currently have a lot of visibility into the collective guidance that our elected officials receive from voters. Without better visibility into this guidance, particularly at the level of our Congressional delegates, none of us are in a position to judge whether our elected officials are carrying out the voters' will directly or using a different standard to guide their actions. Technology exists that would let us aggregate what our fellow voters are saying about priorities and preferences in near real time. In my view, we should deploy this technology on the website of every member of Congress to allow registered voters to input their top priority issues and preferences.

When asked about the possibility of implementing such an initiative, one of my elected officials responded with a concern about voter privacy. I find this objection to be completely off target, but illustrative of the challenge we face. Of course, no system that aggregates voter sentiments has to violate privacy considerations in any way, just as your participation in any of the numerous national polls does not necessarily compromise your privacy. Increasing transparency, however, is not necessarily something all elected officials will want to do.

Much of my analysis decries the power of special interests in our system of government. I want to be clear at the outset that I believe special interests have a valuable and constructive role to play when our system functions as it is designed to function. Unfortunately, insufficient voter participation and modern information technology have allowed the power of special interests, especially political parties, to metastasize to the point where they are a threat to the overall health of our republic. We can quickly and effectively restore a proper balance by improving voter participation or by imposing term limits. Both of these cures de-emphasize the party seniority system.

Either would work. I prefer improved voter participation in the same way a doctor might prefer to cure a medical problem through a change in diet as opposed to surgery.

The book is organized into five chapters: an introduction, a chapter on each of the three elements of the *Accountability Citizenship* paradigm, and a conclusion that discusses the relationship between political participation and the American dream. By necessity, there is some repetition of content between the introduction and the content of the rest of the book. At the end, in an appendix, I provide samples of letters I have written members of Congress as an example of engagement.

I would like to thank the many people who have helped me with this project, directly or indirectly. First, of course, I must thank my family. I am incredibly fortunate to have been born into a family that provided a value-rich environment that encouraged education and service. The debt to my parents and siblings is beyond measure. My family's comments and support have made this book possible and have made it a better product than it otherwise would have been.

I am enormously grateful to the Honorable Max Cleland, former United States Senator and Secretary of the American Battle Monuments Commission. Mr. Cleland is an icon of public service. As a military fellow in his office in the United States Senate in 2000-2001, I observed directly the struggles of a true patriot as he fought for his constituents and for effective government. Countless times, I observed leaders from both political parties lean on Max to elevate hearings and other events above partisanship with his common sense and humor. Indeed, I trace my investigation of the causes and costs of excessive partisanship to this period. I count his mentorship, guidance and friendship among my greatest treasures.

A number of other special friends have read and commented on drafts of this book as it evolved. In particular, I would like to acknowledge the assistance of Dr. Patrick M. Byrne; Colonel Ron Ellis; Colonel Les Knotts, PhD.; Dr. Maren Leed; and Professor Chris Simon (University of Utah). Each of these wonderful people gave generously of their time; each of them significantly improved this book with their insights and comments. Patrick, over decades of conversations, introduced me to a number of texts referenced in this book, including Sowell's *A Conflict of Visions* and Surowiecki's *The Wisdom of Crowds*. Jennifer Cook, Steve Hale, Beth Tryon, Michael Williams, and Ed White also provided valuable observations with the candor that only close friends share. Each of these people improved the quality of my thought and the content of this book. Any errors or omissions in the text, however, are strictly my responsibility.

Finally, I would like to highlight the picture on the cover of the book and explain its relevance to the text. The photo was taken the day I retired from the Army and shows me presenting my three-year-old son with a gift. Explicitly, the gift was a toy action figure of a Soldier from one of the units in which I had served. Implicitly, for me, I want this picture to remind my son that my service itself was the gift—my best effort to leave him a country as strong as the country my parents left me.

I think each of us should view fulfillment of the duties of citizenship as one of the most important gifts we can give to our children and to our communities. Fulfilling the duties of citizenship takes time and effort. Often, no doubt, they conflict with other important responsibilities. *Accountability Citizenship* is an attempt to make some of the tasks associated with the duties of citizenship explicit. We all have to balance, as best we can, the competing requirements of the many important roles we fulfill each day, and none of us will ever be perfectly prepared to vote. But our individual votes may be the most important investments we make in our children's future. If you remember nothing else about this book, remember it as a call to action for every American to vote at every opportunity. In particular, remember it as a call for each of us to communicate our values and priorities to those we elect to represent us in the United States Congress, and to insist on greater transparency with regard to the sentiments expressed by voters in each congressional district.

Stephen Tryon
Salt Lake City, 2013

ONE

Empowering Accountability

"... the common and continual mischiefs of the spirit of party are sufficient to make it the interest and duty of a wise people to discourage and restrain it."

— *George Washington*

Accountability

A few days after Martin Luther King Day last year, I had the privilege of speaking with a group of Chinese officials about America. The Chinese were in the United States studying public policy at the University of Utah, and I was to speak on the relationship between government and business in the United States. As I prepared for the discussion, I focused on how relatively recent legislation, the Sarbanes-Oxley Act of 2002, had come about and how it affected my job as a businessman. The genesis of this legislation was a series of accounting scandals and other incidents of corporate fraud involving multiple large corporations such as Enron. Many trusting people lost money due to these crimes, and a number of senior executives were convicted of wrongdoing. With the Sarbanes-Oxley Act, the Congress of the United States stepped in to improve protection for shareholders by enacting more stringent requirements for corporate accounting practices.

The subject of accountability seemed like an appropriate focal point for the discussion, and the Sarbanes-Oxley Act was a suitable vehicle for discussing the relationship of government and business. The indictment, conviction, and jailing of many senior executives involved in the crimes that led to Sarbanes-Oxley exemplify government holding the convicted business leaders accountable for behaving unethically. Of course, these executives were convicted under laws that were already in effect before Sarbanes-Oxley. The new law was a reaction to the public outrage over the crimes and served to add more rigor to the government's oversight mechanisms. Without a doubt, the law clarified and reinforced the accountability of business leaders for transparent, ethical business practices.

I decided to start the discussion by asserting my belief that to create positive results from any group—in business or government—leaders within the group must create a sense of individual accountability. I used one of my favorite quotations: The French philosopher Voltaire is credited with saying that "No snowflake in an avalanche ever feels responsible." For me, part of the insight in this quotation is that one can *be* responsible without *feeling* responsible. From another perspective, unless we establish the proper accountability at the outset, we can do very bad things together without any one of us feeling like we have done anything wrong individually. In order to create the feeling of individual responsibility, there must be a mechanism for holding individuals accountable. Sarbanes-Oxley formalizes requirements for specific behaviors that should improve individual accountability within corporate hierarchies.

In a wide-ranging discussion that went well beyond the allotted hour, the Chinese officials and I discussed accountability from a number of perspectives including how governments hold other governments accountable for following accepted conventions and laws. I concluded with my belief that the people of a country must hold their government accountable for acting in a way that reflects the values of the people. That conviction lies at the heart of this book. Paradoxically, however, the only way we can hold our government accountable for anything is by holding ourselves accountable for carrying out our duties as citizens—one of the most important of which is the duty to vote.

What I call the information stream here in the United States—traditional media plus the myriad social networking and other information venues in which Americans partake—projects the idea that a majority of us are dissatisfied and frustrated with the United States government. A Gallup poll from October, 2012, shows overall satisfaction at just 30 percent, below the historical rate of 37 percent.[1] A Reason-Rupe poll from September indicated that only 16 percent of respondents approve of the job that Congress,

---

1   http://www.gallup.com/poll/158123

specifically, is doing.[2] Are these shocking levels of dissatisfaction any less urgent than the corporate scandals that galvanized the congressional effort to create Sarbanes-Oxley?

If you are dissatisfied and frustrated with government, then I believe *Accountability Citizenship* offers a solution. Even if you are not in the ranks of the dissatisfied and frustrated, I believe *Accountability Citizenship* offers a way to improve the effectiveness of our government by improving voter participation in government. When Enron collapsed, many trusting Americans were hurt financially. Congress felt broad-based support for immediate action, and the result was the Sarbanes-Oxley Act. Improving voter participation can create broad-based support for congressional action on the many urgent priorities that are causing the astonishing levels of dissatisfaction reflected in recent polls.

Why Don't We Vote?

At the level of individual citizen, we are not fully exercising the power granted us by the Constitution to control our government. The statistical abstract's data set for voter participation in federal elections from 1932 through 2010 indicates a much lower rate of participation, 17 percent lower on average, in non-presidential federal election years than in presidential election years.

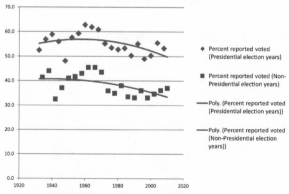

Figure 1: Percent Voting in Presidential Election Years versus Non-Presidential Election Years 1932-2010[13]

Source: U.S. Census Bureau, *The 2012 Statistical Abstract*, Section 7, Table 397, "Participation in Elections for President and U.S. Representatives 1932-2010, p. 244.

2   Reason-Rupe Poll September 13th-17th 2012; http://reason.com/poll

The data shows a general downward trend in participation for both types of federal election beginning around 1972. The passage of the 26th Amendment, which increased the number of eligible voters by lowering the voting age to 18, is the most likely cause for the general downward trend. The addition of a large number of less active voters, however, does not explain the much more severe decrease in participation in non-presidential election years.

The change in voter participation reflected in figure 1 also correlates roughly with both the deregulation of cable television and the beginning of the information and technology explosion we have witnessed over the past four decades. These changes in our information stream may explain the more drastic decrease in voter participation in non-presidential federal election years as compared to presidential election years. In general, Americans have not adapted to the changes in the information stream in the manner necessary to preserve the accountability of the people we elect to serve in Congress.

Certainly the president is the most common face of our government. News media regularly discuss the president's views on major issues and every presidential action is a news story in itself. Not so with Congress. One member of the House of Representatives and two senators represent almost every American citizen in Congress. Yet many of us cannot discuss with certainty how members of our congressional delegation have voted on major issues. Much of what individual members of Congress do is not subject to the same level of media attention that the President gets when he plays golf. It is no surprise that most Americans hold the President accountable for everything the government does or fails to do. But this perception is not consistent with a reasonable assessment of how we should view accountability for our elected federal public servants.

Our Votes for Members of Congress: The Most Powerful Votes We Cast

The fact that more of us vote during national presidential election years reflects a misunderstanding of the relative importance of our votes and our opinions. The relative power of a vote might be measured by the impact of that vote in determining the outcome of an election and in affecting the behavior of the elected official while in office. By both measures, our votes for members of Congress are more powerful than our vote for president.

Our individual votes for members of Congress likely count for more because we elect our congressional delegations directly while our votes for president are mediated by the electoral college. In the electoral college, each state has a number of electors based on population. All states except Maine and Nebraska currently have a winner-take-all system, which means the results of the general election in a state determine which candidate the state's electors support. So if I vote for candidate X and most of the people in my state vote for candidate Y, my state's electors will support candidate Y. My individual vote will not count at all at the national level. The electors from Maine and Nebraska are distributed based on the results of the popular election at the congressional district level. In congressional elections, on the other hand, each individual vote counts directly in determining the final outcome of the election.

We should consider our votes for members of the House of Representatives to be more important than our vote for president for another reason: officials who have to seek reelection more frequently should be more accountable to voters than officials standing for reelection less frequently. Consider the frequency of reelection of members of Congress versus the president. Every representative stands for election every two years. One third of the Senate comes up for election every two years. Presidential elections occur every four years. So for every citizen, the opportunities to vote for federal officials over a six-year period look like the pattern shown in figure 2.

Figure 2: Frequency of Elections for Federal Public Servants

	Representative	Senator 1	Senator 2	President
Year 0	X	X		X
Year 2	X		X	
Year 4	X			X
Year 6	X	X		

On the basis of frequency of reelection, members of the House of Representatives should be the most accountable of all federal elected officials.

Finally, it seems that an official who represents ten people should be more accountable to those ten people than an official who represents five hundred people or five thousand people. The president represents fifty times as many people as the average senator and nearly five hundred times as many people as a member of the House of Representatives. On the basis of the ratio between voters and elected official, our votes for members of the House and Senate should be more powerful than our vote for president.

It is no accident that members of Congress seem to occupy positions that are structurally more accountable than the office of the president. There is ample evidence that the Constitution was written to make Congress—the legislative branch—more powerful and more responsive to the people than the executive branch. The Constitution addresses the legislative branch in Article I, with a few additional clauses throughout the rest of the document. Of the 4,446 words that make up the Constitution, 2,267 words—nearly 51 percent of the document—spell out the powers of the legislative branch. These powers include the sole authority for initiating acts that require expenditure of public funds as well as the authority to approve all presidential appointments. By contrast, only about 1,025 words describe the powers of the executive branch. The facts are that the president is generally able to do only that which has been authorized by Congress, and a majority of voters are not holding members of Congress as accountable as the president for what our government does or fails to do.

Some will argue that we cannot hold individual members of Congress accountable for the outcomes produced by either the 435 representatives in the House or the one hundred senators in the Senate.[3] By this logic, some may consider the president more accountable because he is elected as chief executive and not as a member of a committee. I believe this logic is faulty for two reasons. First, the Constitution gives Congress the role of setting the agenda for the president, and not the other way around. Second, it is not the case that we must hold our representative or senator accountable for

---

3 The problem of holding individuals responsible for collective outcomes is a classic problem of ethical philosophy. In practice, however, we can and do hold individuals accountable for *their part* in collective action. The Enron case is a useful example. We can establish clear measures of effectiveness and accountability for individual members of Congress. To have a fully representative government, we must do so.

the entire corpus of work that is done or not done by the entire Congress. We must only hold them accountable for accomplishing specific, measurable goals we ask them to achieve. To establish individual accountability for members of Congress, we must each communicate reasonable goals and standards to the public servants we elect to the legislative branch. I believe communicating such goals is both possible and necessary. My description of how we each can accomplish this essential task of citizenship comprises much of chapters 2 through 4 of this book.

Usurping Congressional Power: How Special Interests Fill the Accountability Vacuum

Based on the voting behavior described earlier in this chapter, seventeen percent of voters believe their vote for president is more important than their vote for a member of Congress. But we have just seen that it is our members of Congress, not the president, who should be most receptive and accountable for translating the voice of the people into government action. Enter special interests: political parties, unions, associations of all types that represent the vision and values of anything less than a majority of American citizens. By placing too little emphasis on the accountability of individuals in Congress for achieving specific outcomes identified by voters, we set the conditions for special interest groups to exert disproportionate influence on Congress.

The voting behavior depicted in figure 1 undermines congressional accountability to the people that Congress is supposed to serve by allowing candidates for Congress to run based on ideological alignment rather than on the merits of specific policies, programs and positions they endorse. When candidates are accountable only for their ideological alignment, the relative power of political parties and other special interest groups increases because advertising dollars become more important than specific behaviors. To see how this works, we must return to the data in figure 1. Less than forty percent of voting-age residents vote in non-presidential election years. The default measure of success for a member of Congress, therefore, is to convince the people who *will* vote in the next election—most of whom likely are people at either end of the political spectrum—that the member's campaign promises are better than the promises of others in the race.

Since people running for office have to address only a small population of relatively committed voters, incumbents and candidates can run successful campaigns with campaign promises that lack specific content. The relatively committed voters whom candidates must address are generally more concerned about ideological alignment than about the content of specific policies, positions, and promises. Our vote for Congressman X becomes a vote against the other party's agenda more than a vote for any concrete actions or policies. Or, if it is a vote for some policy, it is at a level of abstraction that does not allow for true accountability. Depending on our political orientation, we vote for candidates who promise to stop wasteful spending or to make corporations and the wealthy pay more in taxes. These positional promises are too vague: to hold individual members of Congress accountable we must elicit promises or behaviors that are specific and measurable.

If we are not holding individual members responsible for achieving specific outcomes, the content of campaign promises becomes less important than the quantity and quality of advertising that an incumbent or candidate can afford. Congressional elections become little more than advertising contests. The incumbent or candidate who has the best communication plan generally wins. Communications plans cost money, and the most effective communication plan generally costs the most money. Individual citizens are not able to provide as much money or promise as many votes as political parties, associations and other interest groups.

Currently, political parties and other interest groups are better able to use their contributions to influence the behavior of members of Congress than are the individual citizens whom the members represent. The set of social and technological changes that have led to what we call the age of information have made powerful tools available for those organized to use those tools. Interest groups typically have a budget and one or more people dedicated to strategic communications: crafting and positioning messages to have the most powerful effect in furthering the goals of the organization. But the goals of the many and varied groups that compete for power and influence within our government are not representative of the will of the majority of the people as individual citizens. Furthermore, in aggregate, the goals of the multitude of special interests are often not consistent with what is best for our country.

In his farewell address, President George Washington spoke at length about the dangers to our liberty posed by special interests. Washington's warnings about the dangers of special interests—what he called factions— seem incredibly prescient today. Washington wrote, "All combinations and associations, under whatever plausible character… serve to organize faction, to give it an artificial and extraordinary force; to put, in the place of the delegated will of the nation the will of a party, often a small but artful and enterprising minority of the community; and, according to the alternate triumphs of different parties, to make the public administration the mirror of the ill-concerted and incongruous projects of faction, rather than the organ of consistent and wholesome plans digested by common counsels and modified by mutual interests."[4] One of the strongest themes in the final public message from the Father of our Country was this stern warning against the dangers of political parties and other special interests.

Special interest groups use their power to influence the only branch of our government with the constitutional authority to appropriate public money—Congress. As long as special interest groups or the people associated with them are getting the results that they want—mostly in the form of public money being spent as they wish—they are perfectly happy to maintain things as they are. By definition, however, special interests are groups that optimize outcomes for a subset of our republic, not for our republic as a whole. In fact, there is good reason to believe, as George Washington believed, that optimization of special interests is harmful to our republic overall.

The voting trends shown in figure 1 allow members of Congress to escape individual accountability for whatever Congress as a whole does or fails to do. This in turn allows interest groups to exercise disproportionate influence on the branch of government designed to amplify the voice of the people. The data shows an increasing tendency on the part of individual citizens to disregard the most effective vehicle we have for controlling the direction of our government.

Restoring Accountability: Putting the Quarter in the Jar

I believe Americans have to restore individual accountability in our political system, especially in Congress. I want to suggest two simple steps to achieve this objective. First, we have to acknowledge our individual accountability as citizens for everything our government does or fails to do. Second, we have

---

4   George Washington, "Farewell Address," 1796, transcript, *The Avalon Project: Documents in Law, History, and Diplomacy,* Lillian Goldman Law Library, Yale Law School, http://avalon.law.yale.edu/18th_century/washing.asp.

to establish clear accountability for specific behaviors that we expect from each official we elect to public office, especially our members of Congress. Neither of these steps is particularly difficult at the individual level if we create tangible, daily tasks to inform our understanding of what government is doing as well as our vision for what government should be doing.

When we want to change a personal habit, we often make a resolution. People sometimes use what I will refer to as the "jar technique" to help them with such resolutions. The resolver enlists friends to help identify when she has violated the resolution, and she agrees to put a quarter in a jar every time a violation occurs. Creating this artificial tax on the behavior one is trying to change helps make the desired change in behavior a tangible part of our everyday routine.

Accountability Citizenship is one way of applying the jar technique to the routine tasks we should be performing as American citizens living in the information age. We have to vote, empower those around us to vote, and make our friends put a quarter in the jar when they fail to vote. We have to work at being informed, in a balanced way, and we have to make others put a quarter in the jar when they fail to acknowledge the fundamental dignity and reason of those with whom they disagree. We have to be active consumers of information and government, and put a quarter in the jar each time we find ourselves passively accepting the verdict of the information stream without sufficient evidence.

To be sure, what I am prescribing is a departure from the way American citizens have traditionally behaved. For most of our history, we have been passive consumers of information and government. I leave it to the reader to assess our history, as I have done in chapter three, and decide whether that has been good enough. *Accountability Citizenship* suggests that our information stream has recently evolved, and that American citizens today have to adapt to that change if we are to preserve our system of government.

The Second Step: Performance Management for Elected Officials

If we follow the prescription of *Accountability Citizenship*, we will find it easy to establish clear accountability on the part of our elected officials. This step is no different than the performance management systems most of us experience in our jobs. Elected officials work for us. They are not royalty, though we tend to treat them that way. We, the people, are their supervisors.

It is up to us to establish clear, measurable performance objectives for each of the individuals for whom we vote. It is up to us to evaluate whether those we elect have adequately acknowledged, synthesized, and achieved the objectives we set for them.

In this book, I focus extensively on our personal relationship with the three members of Congress who represent each of us.[5] In spite of how we may feel about Congress today, the Constitution clearly establishes Congress as the avenue through which we, the people, can most quickly and dramatically change the behavior of our government. If you do not believe this is the case, consider this fact: if we all chose to replace our current members of Congress at every opportunity, we could replace 87 percent of the members of Congress every two years. If we feel that Congress is gridlocked, it can only be because we, the people, have failed to communicate with our votes that gridlock is not acceptable.

At this point, some will undoubtedly object that we do not have enough information to hold members of Congress accountable in the manner I believe we should. If that is the case, then I suggest that we have not made our members of Congress accountable for providing us the information that we need. Every member of Congress has a web site that is paid for with tax dollars. Technology exists today to allow each registered voter in a district or state to go on to a member's web site and quickly rank in order the issues and positions the voter considers most important. Technology exists today to display an anonymous summary of the voter priorities submitted in this way. Given this technology, we could all see what the voters in our districts and states are asking our members of Congress to do. The fact that our members of Congress are not making use of available technology to create a fully transparent relationship with their constituents is a failure on our part to demand this level of service.

The Information Stream, Political Awareness, and Voting Behavior

We are swimming in information. From the moment we are awake until we go to sleep, we are inundated with information from radio, television,

---

5   I note that citizens living in the District of Columbia do not have equal representation. The District of Columbia was created to provide a location for federal legislators to work without being subject to the jurisdiction of any state delegation.

newspapers, magazines, tweets, blogs, flyers, billboards, e-mail, and junk mail. Taken together, all of this is what I call the information stream.

The content of the stream is not universally coherent. As the sources of information have proliferated, so has the content itself. On the one hand, this has improved access to a wide variety of specialized information. With just a few keystrokes, one can find entire websites devoted to the most arcane pursuits. On the other hand, news outlets catering to national audiences specialize in presenting information at the level that will appeal to the broadest audience. Local outlets, and the stories that focus more on the activities and priorities of local congressional delegations, compete with a much larger set of available information. To a greater extent than ever before, voters have to seek out the information needed to establish and maintain a value-rich accountability connection with the members of their congressional delegation.

How did we get here? I believe the free press—unfettered by any form of censorship except that absolutely necessary to preserve the individual rights and safety of others—is indispensable to sustaining our republic. With information age technology, however, traditional media has evolved into an information industry quite different than anything envisioned in the early days of our nation's history. Then media consisted largely of newspapers, and it was largely a local phenomenon. Thus it was much more likely to be concerned with local perspectives and the role of individual members of a congressional delegation than with strictly national or global news. In other words, media aimed at a local audience because that audience provided the subscription base on which the newspaper businesses relied. Newspapers, therefore, served as a relatively independent accountability broker for individual members of Congress and their constituents.

Technology and time have industrialized media just as it has other means of production. The lines have blurred between traditional media and companies specializing in advertising, entertainment and other forms of communication. Today, these enterprises mass produce and package information for popular consumption by the largest possible audience because that is how the information-age media and communications *business* maximizes its profits. Media businesses make money not only through subscriptions but also, and in many cases primarily, from clients—often organizations with advertising staffs and budgets—that pay to have special advertising and messaging included in the information stream. In the process of mass producing information for the broadest possible audience, today's information industry tends to be more national or global and less local.

The industry no longer functions as an independent accountability broker because its economic incentives are no longer primarily driven by the subscriptions of individual consumers. Rather, media outlets are part of an industry that produces the information stream. That information stream is a blend of what will attract the broadest audience and what the industry's clients want to project. If we are passive consumers of this information stream—absorbing the sensations presented to us without applying a positive structure—then the amount of information and the manner in which it is presented are confusing and tend to alienate us from the issues most relevant to our relationship with our members of Congress.

Passive consumers of a special-interest-driven information stream are bombarded with an overwhelming volume of messages from a wide variety of sources. The individual messages themselves are not necessarily coordinated to mislead or deceive anyone. However, the communications industry uses the psychology of the audience as a way of crafting messages that will be most effective in getting people to take whatever specific action the messages promote. Behavioral science and the science of crafting effective advertising, therefore, coalesce around a series of communications techniques that tend to strike the same emotional and psychological chords.

Remember, the information industry uses information as a way of generating profit. To create profit from information, information businesses compete for consumers. These businesses get consumers by generating an overwhelming and inescapable stream of information—something for everyone—and by packaging information in ways consumers find appealing. Controversy, sex, conflict and the appeal to fear sell better than facts alone.

Psychologically and structurally, the media industry sensationalizes information by appealing to subjects that excite and interest viewers. The sex lives of celebrities, corporate scandals, environmental disasters, and the state of the economy here and abroad compete with traditional political topics for a spot in the information stream. These topics interest readers, viewers, and surfers; but they also dilute information about the political behavior of specific members of Congress. The political news that is present—even in local programs and venues—is often packaged from the national perspective: the general conflict between political parties takes precedence over reporting on specific behaviors of individual members of the local congressional delegation because the more general content appeals to a broader audience. Passive consumers of the information stream no longer get the information they need to be the primary drivers of government accountability.

It is correct to note that sensationalism and conflict-oriented media have been with us to some degree throughout our history. The phenomenon was labeled "yellow journalism" at the close of the 19th century, when it came into focus as major American newspapers competed to increase their circulation. However, I believe social and technological trends that have emerged over the past half century make certain aspects of the media industry particularly corrosive to government accountability.

First, of course, the information industry today spans far more than just newspapers. The marketing dollars attached to readership, viewership, and most recently, "clicks" on the Internet have grown enormously since Pulitzer battled Hearst for the subscriptions of New York newspaper readers. The lure of staying connected now extends beyond newspapers, magazines, radio, television, and personal computers to our mobile phones. The technological advances that allow us to stream news live to our phones have intensified the effects of the media industry in the information cycle. We are immersed in information from the moment we wake until we go to sleep. Passive consumers of information experience life through a commercialized information filter that can condition our thoughts and feelings.

Second, to achieve scale needed to optimize profit, the media industry has homogenized its content to appeal to the broadest possible audience. In concrete terms, we see more coverage of concerns and scandals appealing to national and global audiences than stories with the detail needed to maintain local accountability of our elected public servants. Media tends to focus more on the president than on Congress. Coverage of Congress tends to orient more on political parties than on the behaviors of individual members. We are conditioned to view the political landscape in terms of Democrats, Republicans, and the president. As passive consumers of information, we do not get the detail relevant to our role as individual voters responsible for the behavior of a specific subset of congressional representatives.

Our two-party system resonates with the conflict-debate orientation of the media. Officials attempt to sway public opinion using the media, and the media feeds on the conflict between the party positions. The two systems reinforce one another in ways that seem to make compromise almost undesirable. Political figures become more accountable for sustaining the positions they have adopted publically than for modifying those positions in ways that might better serve our republic as a whole. Thus we have deadlocks over budgets that extend to the last possible moment, only to be told that "last possible moment" really wasn't the last possible moment. The drama renews itself as we prepare for the next "last possible moment." Passive consumers of information can't help but feel cynical about the honesty of elected public servants and the people who report on them.

I want to be absolutely clear: I believe this condition has evolved because of our collective failure to adapt to the modern information environment. It is not a result of some grand conspiracy on the part of malicious media moguls or politicians or even evil lobbyists. Imagine waking up in the middle of winter and finding the temperature in our house falling steadily. We know instinctively how to address this physical aspect of our environment: we put another log on the fire, turn up the heat, and cover ourselves with more blankets. In recent decades, the information component of our environment has changed dramatically. We recognize the change and even refer to our times as the information age. But the individual and social response to this phenomenon is not instinctive. In fact, I doubt many people even consider the information environment as something to which we need to respond as individuals. But living in the information stream that surrounds us today without adequate preparation is like going to the beach without sunscreen. The difference is that we can see and feel the effects of the sun over time while we fail to recognize the damaging effects of passive exposure to a special-interest-driven information stream.

Voter Dysfunction, Special Interests, and Accountability

The lack of constituent engagement with government, and especially with Congress, is a serious departure from the way our government was designed to function. Judging simply from the weight of words in our Constitution, it seems as if Congress was intended to be the main vehicle for translating the vision and values of the American people into government policy and action. The Constitution devotes twice as much of its content to defining congressional powers and responsibilities as it does to defining presidential powers and responsibilities. In particular, the Constitution vests Congress with the power of the purse: expenditures of public funds must generally be appropriated by Congress, and all bills for raising revenue have to originate from the House of Representatives. For this reason alone, the decrease in voter engagement with Congress has created a dangerous vacuum, which has naturally been filled by special interests seeking disbursements of public funds or modifications to the tax law for many and varied causes.

I want to say again that I am not proposing any grand conspiracy of special interests. Rather, my thesis is that there has been a change in our society to which we have failed to respond, and that our failure to respond has allowed some harmful trends and practices to take root. Our collective failure to adapt to the modern information stream has put our elected public servants in a tough spot. I believe most representatives and senators go to Washington with the best intentions to improve government. They find, however, that they must compete for the financial support they need to win the next election.[6] The financial support they need is provided by special interests, including all of our political parties.[7] Politicians need money to buy placement in the information stream—they use special interest money to create their "brand."

As a consequence, politicians in general are more accountable to special interests than to their constituents. It is easy for well-intentioned elected officials to justify the behaviors needed to stay in office by telling themselves that their reelection will help them gain the power to make meaningful changes. Those who fail to adequately support political parties and other special interests are likely targeted—or at least not supported—in the information stream. They face an uphill battle in the next election. Elected officials can't serve our country as well as they should because most of us do not vote. Furthermore, many who do vote, including the officials themselves, have been conditioned by a special-interest-driven information stream that distorts government policies and programs in dysfunctional ways.

The Wisdom of Crowds, Cooperation, and the American Dream

In *The Wisdom of Crowds,* James Surowiecki argues that given certain conditions, the average solution of a group will often be superior to that of the individuals in the group. The group solution is often better than those of the most well-informed individuals in the group. Surowiecki examines three types of issues. Cognition issues are those that have or will have definitive solutions such as picking the horse that will win the Kentucky Derby. Coordination issues are those in which group members have to

---

6   A number of the members of Congress with whom I worked from 2000–2004 chafed at the requirement for raising funds.

7   George Washington warned us in his farewell address more than two hundred years ago that political parties are the most potent and dangerous special interests. Washington, "Farewell Address."

coordinate individual behaviors with the understanding that everyone else is trying to do the same thing. Driving in traffic is one of the examples cited in the book. Finally, cooperation issues "involve the challenge of getting self-interested, distrustful people to work together, even when narrow self-interest would seem to dictate that no individual should take part."[8] Paying taxes is one of the examples the author cites to illustrate a cooperation issue. Voter participation would seem to be another cooperation issue.

Surowiecki identifies three conditions necessary for successful group decision making: diversity, independence, and decentralization. "Collective decisions are most likely to be good ones when they're made by people with diverse opinions reaching independent conclusions, relying primarily on their private information."[9] These conditions support the idea that the level of voter participation is important to the quality of an election's results. Therefore, we should try to reverse the trend of decreasing voter participation. Likewise, we should encourage people to vote in accordance with their best judgment rather than worrying about the opinions of others or about who is expected to win.

In his discussion of how the group intelligence phenomenon operates in the context of cooperation problems, Surowiecki illustrates that the perception of fairness and the degree to which people who behave unfairly are punished are key underpinnings of cooperative groups.[10] In general, people consider outcomes as fair as long as any disparities correlate (both quantitatively and qualitatively) with the perceived qualifications of the individuals receiving the most rewards. Given no other information, individuals accept some cost to themselves to enforce fairness. Most behave fairly themselves as long as they perceive others are also behaving fairly. Over time, with the perception that unfair behavior is going unpunished, the level of social cooperation drops. These features of group decision-making for cooperation problems encourage careful attention to issues of fairness and to the accuracy of commonly held biases or myths projected by the information stream. They support the notion that any perception of undue influence by special interests might be particularly corrosive to voting behaviors.

Surowiecki presents some interesting contrasts between beliefs about fairness in Europe and in the United States. For instance, "Americans are

---

8   James Surowiecki, The Wisdom of Crowds (New York: Anchor Books, 2005), xiii–xviii.
9   Ibid. 57.
10 Ibid., 108–42.

far more likely to believe that wealth is the result of initiative and skill, while Europeans are far more likely to attribute it to luck."[11] The author also asserts that Americans have a higher tolerance for disparities in wealth and pay their taxes at a higher rate than Europeans. Surowiecki connects some of these ideas to the common belief in the possibility of social mobility in the United States.[12] This collective faith in the ability of any person to become wealthy through persistence and hard work is what many refer to as the American dream. It would seem that our belief in the United States as a land of opportunity is instrumental to the level of cooperative behavior—like paying taxes and voting—in our society.

Accountability Citizenship argues that the level of non-voting behavior in the United States undermines the individual accountability of our elected federal officials, especially members of Congress. In fact, current trends encourage federal elected officials to be more accountable to special interests than to individual constituents. When special interests are first in line, the perception of unfairness is likely to grow. Such a perception might manifest itself as dissatisfaction and frustration with government. Under these circumstances, we could expect the cooperative behaviors—voting, paying of taxes, etc.,—to decay, making the challenges facing our government progressively worse.

Accountability Citizenship

This book is my prescription for Americans to reestablish control of our government using the procedures provided in our Constitution. I believe our solutions lie not in changing the information stream—the free press is an inviolable element of our republic—but rather in changing our behaviors for processing the information that the stream conveys. My recipe calls for each of us to adopt behaviors necessary for effective information-age citizenship by becoming active rather than passive consumers of information. In this age of information, we have to hold each other accountable —private citizen and elected official alike—for adopting information-age behaviors in order to preserve a government that represents the will of the people.

In the United States, more than in any other place in the world, if our government is not performing as we want it to perform, we have no one

---

11 Ibid., 115.
12 Ibid.,115, 141.

to blame but ourselves. It is not the case that our government is a thing apart from us. Our government is a direct reflection of the values we have communicated or failed to communicate. It is an institution made up of our friends and neighbors. It is an institution completely within our power to fix once enough of us begin to vote and to communicate with the people we elect to represent us.

My purpose in writing this book is to explain how we can restore the accountability of the federal public servants we elect by accepting our personal accountability for some simple tasks we must do as individual citizens living in the age of information. I intend the book to be nonpartisan. We only have to agree on the very basics—that the government of the United States is supposed to represent the people of the United States.

The Declaration of Independence states that governments derive their power from the consent of the people. It further asserts that governments exist to secure unalienable rights of life, liberty and the pursuit of happiness. The preamble to our Constitution states the purpose of that document is to "form a more perfect Union, establish Justice, insure domestic Tranquility, provide for the common defense, promote the general Welfare, and secure the Blessings of Liberty to ourselves and our Posterity."[13] We don't have to agree on the specifics of what these words mean. The people who wrote and approved these words disagreed on their precise meaning.[14] But they agreed on the principle that the government of the United States is supposed to represent the people of the United States. If we can agree to that principle and if we are willing to apply a few techniques of information-age citizenship in our own lives, we can leverage basic time management, critical reasoning, and performance management to empower our elected public servants to do their jobs.

I call my prescription "accountability citizenship" because each of us is *responsible* for what our government does or fails to do. We should therefore be *accountable* for what our government does or fails to do. We should hold each other accountable for practicing voter behaviors that align government action with our collective values. As accountable citizens, we should be appropriately positive, appropriately informed, and appropriately engaged.

Being appropriately positive means taking positive control of the

---

13 *The Declaration of Independence and the Constitution of the United States,* U.S. Department of Homeland Security http://publications.usa.gov/USAPubs. php?PubID=1331
14 Joseph Ellis, *Founding Brothers* (New York: Vintage Books, 2002), 78.

information stream as it confronts us each day through the application of basic time management skills. This makes us active rather than passive consumers of information. Being appropriately informed is a disciplined use of available information and basic critical reasoning skills to achieve an informed, balanced perspective on the issues. Being appropriately engaged means applying the information we absorb to vote, to communicate our values, and to scorecard the performance of our elected public servants. In this way, we empower ourselves to establish and preserve the accountability of our elected officials for the reasonable, tangible outcomes we value most highly. In subsequent chapters, I will expand on these elements of accountability citizenship.

Accountability for What?

When I first described to friends and family my model for restoring accountability to government, some asked the question, "Accountability for what?" The point of the question, of course, is that many of us have quite different ideas of what constitutes good government. Empowering citizens to hold officials accountable for each citizen's individual ideas might not get us anywhere.

The authors of the Declaration of Independence and the Constitution of the United States along with those who have crafted the twenty-seven amendments to the Constitution, and those who continue to interpret this body of work in laws like the Civil Rights Act and judicial decisions like *Roe v. Wade*, have established a balance between individual liberties and societal constraints on those liberties. It is this balance that comprises our current social contract. We don't all agree with every aspect of the contract in its current form. The power of our social contract lies just as much in the mechanisms for peacefully modifying its content as in any particular provision, law, or court decision.

It is not the purpose of this book to debate the particulars of the contract in its current form. I understand that we don't all agree about whether *Roe v. Wade* is correct or about the limits of the Second Amendment. I understand that some of us are Democrats and some of us are Republicans and some of us are Libertarians or independents or some other thing. It is not my purpose in this book to advocate for any particular party or position over any other. I intend to stay at a level of generality that allows what I have to say about accountability to apply to all citizens.

But I think the question "Accountability for what?" reinforces one point I want to make: a significant element of the job description for our members of Congress should be to synthesize the views of the people who elect them. Of course, the synthesis will not satisfy everyone, and members will have to represent their districts on matters beyond the specific guidance they have received. But the synthesis should happen in the persons of our elected representative and senators. And if we each communicate our vision and values for government to our representatives, and our members of Congress clearly communicate back that for which they believe themselves accountable, we should each be able to decide whether any given member of Congress deserves our vote in the next election.

Elected officials must synthesize our input. They must communicate back the set of specific behaviors they will pursue to represent us. We must be engaged in managing and evaluating their performance. We will not all agree all of the time. But if we all exercise accountability citizenship, I believe we will find the consensus that emerges is much more coherent and wholesome than what we are led to believe as passive consumers of a special-interest-driven information stream.

To be clear, then, my answer to the question, "Accountability for what?" is that we must all hold each other accountable for voting in every election because our independent participation as voters is what makes our system work. Together, we must hold each elected official, especially the individual members of Congress who represent each of us, accountable for representing the people they serve. Each of us decides and communicates for ourselves that for which we will hold our elected officials accountable.

What's My Motivation Here?

Why is it important for each of us to apply accountability citizenship and assert the power granted us in the Constitution to control our House of Representatives, our Senate, and our government? The answer to this question is that accountability citizenship is the best way to restore the personal accountability of our elected officials for the results of government action and inaction. The absence of personal accountability for group outcomes allows groups and leaders to justify actions that no group member would support. Groups justify behaviors inconsistent with the values of group members by appealing to abstractions such as the interest of the group as a whole or the "greater good."

Our government represents the largest economy in the world and commands the most powerful military in the world. Without individual accountability, our government will act to achieve and preserve optimal outcomes for the special interests to which it is most responsive. We must insist on strict personal accountability of elected public servants for the collective actions of our government, or we risk the irresponsible use of governmental authority in a way that is harmful to large numbers of our fellow citizens, to the innocent citizens of other countries, and to our republic itself. However we have gotten to this place, where many of us seem to misplace accountability in the executive branch while special interests usurp the accountability of Congress, we must recognize that these current trends create a dangerous gap between what we want and what the government does.

We can reverse these trends by adopting a set of information-age citizen behaviors I call accountability citizenship. Accountability citizenship requires that we shift from being passive to active consumers of information and government. We become active consumers by being appropriately positive, appropriately informed, and appropriately engaged. Applying a positive structure of personal priorities and basic time management principles—being appropriately positive—inoculates us from the negative effects of information overload. Basic information processing skills and a rudimentary appreciation of our history and government enables us to be appropriately informed—to absorb important information from the free press while compensating for the bias of the special-interest-driven information stream. Being appropriately positive and appropriately informed empowers each of us to be appropriately engaged with our government—engaged in a way that restores and sustains an acceptable level of accountability. This systematic approach to individual citizenship, reinvented a bit for the information age, is all that is required to restore the full power of the American ideal of government of the people, by the people, and for the people. Now more than ever, in the information age, accountability citizenship is important. If we use it to restore the individual accountability of those we elect to Congress, we will benefit ourselves, our country, and the other countries with which we share the world and its resources.

Two

Being Appropriately Positive

"No free government, nor the blessings of liberty, can be preserved to any people, but by... a frequent recurrence to fundamental principles."

— *George Mason, 1776*

Being appropriately positive means building and managing a positive structure or filter with which to engage the information stream. Adopting a positive posture makes us active rather than passive consumers of information. As active consumers, we use time management to selectively engage the information stream and get complete, balanced information on our top priority issues. We use survey techniques to detect new issues and trends in the information stream. We actively assess, rather than passively accept, subtle messages the information stream projects that may be more information marketing than truth. Finally, we contribute our perspective to inform the behaviors of our elected officials. Together, these practices protect us from being misled by the rhetoric that is used to sell information.

Using Time Management

The first step to being appropriately positive is to create a list of our top priority issues and our beliefs about how government should address those issues.

We may engage in some research at the outset to inform this process, or the process may simply reflect our current understanding of our government and current events. Regardless of the technique we use to develop our list, the most important thing is for each of us to capture in writing the things we consider most important—essentially this is the statement of vision and values by which we should each measure the performance of our federal elected officials.

The political courage test sponsored by Votesmart.org is a terrific starting point for this deliberation. The test is a nonpartisan, standardized method for capturing the vision and values of elected officials regarding a generic slate of the most talked-about issues facing our society and our government. The sixteen issues in the *2012 Congressional Edition* are organized alphabetically and include topics such as Afghanistan, campaign finance, energy, environment, health care, and social security. The section on spending and taxes asks candidates to state how they would change funding for major elements of the budget, and provides a space for candidates to add elements not included in the test. A similar ranking asks candidates to provide their vision for how they would change taxes. Finally, the test provides space for candidates to state, in 100 words or less, their "top two or three priorities if elected."[15] The simplest way for each of us to develop our personal list of priorities for federal elected officials is to take the test ourselves, modifying it as we see fit.

A clear sense of our individual vision and values enables us to apply time management principles to master the overwhelming volume of information which confronts us all. It enables us to actively search for information on issues that are priorities for us. The process of actively searching for information takes us from being a target for the messages others want us to see to being in control of how we process information. Actively searching for information in accordance with our individual priority list will likely force us to confront new and different sources of information and opinions. Initially, we may find that we do not have enough time to cover every topic on our list. But by working in priority order and limiting our high priority list, we empower ourselves to spend an adequate amount of time to gain an informed, mature perspective on the issues we consider most important first. Over time, as we become more familiar with the resources available to aid our information search, we become more efficient and are able to cover more topics.

---

15   Project Vote Smart, "The Political Courage Test," 2012 Congressional Ed., http://votesmart.org/static/pdf/2012/pct/2012_Cong_Political_Courage_Test.pdf

Equipped with our list of priority issues, we actively seek information about the things that concern us most. To start with, we must use some standard to ensure we get enough information to provide a balanced view of our priorities. Without such a standard, we risk using our list merely as a way of cementing our preconceived opinions about issues without really becoming better informed on those issues.

The standard I prefer is to identify some public person with political affiliations opposite my own and then research the statements and views of that person with respect to my high priority issue. I like this technique because it is relatively easy to identify a prominent politician from the opposing political camp. If you consider yourself neutral politically, then it is useful to research the statements and views of prominent officials from each of the major parties. For instance, you could simply identify the House minority leader and the speaker of the House as the two politicians likely to have opposite views on most issues. These are the two positions held by the leaders of the opposing political parties in the House of Representatives. If you do not know the name of the person currently serving in one or both of those roles, you may find this information on the web site for the House of Representatives, House.gov.

Once you have identified the people whose views you choose to survey, it is a simple matter to search for what those people have said about the issue in question. You should read the views of these political figures as they have expressed those views, not as their views have been summarized by others. If I read the views of a liberal political figure as it is summarized by a conservative source (or vice versa), the presentation of views will almost certainly be slanted in a negative way. Thus, to survey both sides of an issue fairly, you should read the views of political figures in statements or speeches the figures themselves have approved. You can also use Votesmart.org as a nonpartisan source of information on the issue positions of specific elected officials. In the next chapter, we will discuss other techniques for ensuring we adequately survey the range of perspectives on our high priority issues.

Surveying the Information Stream

Too much emphasis on using our list of priority issues merely as a filter can prevent us from seeing emerging issues and trends, so we need to incorporate a survey technique into our model for being an active consumer of information. The survey technique I prefer is to scan the front pages of several different newspapers and the table of contents of different magazines. Electronic versions of newspapers and magazines make this easier than ever. Public libraries are good sources for finding a variety of newspapers and magazines without having to pay for multiple subscriptions. The web site for Project Vote Smart also contains good summaries of current events and attempts to present both sides of emerging issues.

For me, scanning the front page of a newspaper or an article in a magazine means more than just reading the headlines, which I find somewhat misleading at times. Instead, I prefer to read at least the first paragraph of each story. If I do not feel I understand the story at that point then I also read the last paragraph of the article. If an article covers a topic that I have identified on my list of high priority issues, I will read the entire article. The intent is to read quickly, gaining an understanding of the main idea of the article without laboring over every idea. Remember, the purpose of this scan is to ensure we are familiar with emerging issues so we can modify our list of priorities for further research if appropriate.

Creating a positive structure for processing information is the first step to being appropriately positive. Defining a list of priority issues, structuring our research to ensure we review a range of opinions, and incorporating a survey technique to keep us abreast of emerging issues are key steps to creating a positive structure. These steps are basically an application of time management principles to make us more efficient, and *active*, consumers of information.

Questioning Subtle Messaging

Effective time management is not the only benefit of positive structure. By deciding on a finite set of issues and criteria by which to assess the performance of our elected public servants, we protect ourselves somewhat from being manipulated by those who pay to shape the information stream. If I can pay to flood your information stream with information I want to promote, and you are not actively managing your information flow, then I can distract you from focusing on other information about other topics. Depending on how persuasive or engaging my information is, you may be disturbed by this process of distraction. Furthermore, since I am likely crafting my message using principles of consumer psychology, my message probably coalesces with others around some basic general themes. The point here is that the basic themes embedded within the information stream are often used because those themes have a psychological effect, not because the themes accurately depict the world.

I find that the information stream tends to project at least five messages—I call them the five myths—that tend to increase voter apathy and a general sense of hopelessness among passive consumers of the stream.

- The *conspiracy myth* assigns the blame for some social ill to a conspiracy of some specific subset of the population.
- The *quality myth* asserts that Americans today are not as smart, enterprising, or honest as Americans of the past.
- The *accountability myth* tells us that individual members of Congress are powerless to change a system that seems stuck between dysfunction and gridlock.
- The *complexity myth* tells us that the problems and issues we face are so complex that they exceed the capacity of average citizens to resolve.
- The *polarization myth* tells us that our country faces overwhelming problems which have polarized our systems and citizens to the point that we can't agree on solutions.

Passive consumers of information are left with a lingering sense of despair: a sense that nothing we do as individuals will arrest the decay of our society as projected by the stream. I should emphasize at the outset that I believe the myths emerge from the nature of the information industry and our psychology as consumers of information, not from any systemic intent to mislead on the part of communications professionals.

In the following paragraphs, I do not intend to prove these themes false. In fact, I doubt that any of them are completely true or completely false. However, I want to make a plausible case for the notion that the themes are present because they attract viewers and readers rather than because they are accurate descriptions of our society. I want to make the case that each of us should actively assess the truth of these themes. As we view current events through the lens of these myths, we tend to adopt a perspective that is more negative than what we might adopt based on facts alone. Widespread, passive acceptance of the myths undermines our willingness to do routine tasks of citizenship necessary to sustain truly representative government.

The conspiracy myth, for example, generally assigns blame for a given problem by inferring a conscious, active effort on the part of some group to create that problem. I believe it is generally wrong to infer such a conspiracy for two main reasons. First, the "groups" to which we tend to assign blame are usually categories of people rather than true associations unified for some common purpose. Second, even when the groups we suspect of conspiracy are truly associations of people with common purpose, the purpose they endorse is usually intended to solve a problem rather than to intentionally create one. Let us consider each of my objections in turn.

Our instinct to infer a conspiracy may be wrong because the groups we tend to blame are often categories of people rather than true associations unified for common purpose. I have written at length, for instance, about the harmful effects of special interest groups. I do not believe, however, that there is a conspiracy of special interests. The harmful effects, about which I have written, *emerge* from the cumulative activity of independent groups all trying to achieve specific goals for some cause they endorse.

Likewise, even when the groups we blame are truly associations with a common purpose, it is unlikely that they aspire to do something that hurts our government or our country. Lobbyists, for instance, are often singled out as a cause of inefficiency and corruption in government. Subsets of this group, linked by common purpose because they represent the same company or industry, may well coordinate their activities in order to influence legislation in specific ways. But these lobbyists likely do not consider their activities to be harmful to government efficiency or ethics. Rather, they probably consider themselves to be providing information in order to legitimately optimize a specific outcome in a way that contributes to good governance.

I might even take this a step further: given an adequate level of voter participation, the efforts of these various groups might increase the effectiveness of our government. Such coordinated efforts appear as conspiracies only because they gain disproportionate effect when more than half of voting-age residents opt out of our election processes. Ascribing a negative motive to the collective efforts of others is a ready-made excuse for inaction. We justify our own failure to vote, or to write our representatives in Congress, because we lose faith that our individual effort can make a difference against the imagined conspiracy. The overall level of voter apathy and inaction may be the real source of the problems we project onto the activities of others by labeling them conspiracies.

Buying into the myth that Americans today are not as smart, enterprising, or honest as Americans of the past can also make us feel hopeless. After all, if it is the case that our modern society has made us all softer and lazier and less able to triumph over adversity than previous generations, what is the use of any one of us striving to make things better? The problem with this myth is that it has inductive form, reasoning from specific cases to support a broader conclusion. An opposing thesis appears plausible with a different selection of examples.

Furthermore, one could argue that our social awareness of specific behaviors of individuals has grown exponentially over the past two hundred years. Thus, the nostalgic view that Americans were somehow better in the good old days might have more to do with the fact that an individual's circle of awareness was significantly smaller before the advent of high-tech information systems. In other words, we think we were better way back then because the subset of people who cared enough to reflect and comment on such matters could only observe a relatively small number of like-minded fellow citizens. Had observers been able to observe the behavior of a larger sample of the population in the earliest days of our republic, it may well be the case they would have recorded patterns of vice and virtue similar to what we see today.

Even with perfect information, what would the quality myth have to mean in order to be significant? The census of 1790 reported the population of the United States at about four million. This is just 1.3 percent of the nearly 309 million reported in the census of 2010. It is hard to imagine that the top 1.3 percent of our population today would not compare favorably to the entire population of the early United States in terms of industriousness or creativity or any other dimension one might care to measure.

The thesis of this book is that the behavior of Americans today as passive consumers of information has not kept pace with the behavioral requirements of effective citizenship in the information age. But this is not a claim that American citizens are better or worse than they were in previous generations. In fact, my thesis is most clear if you assume that the intellectual and moral quality of American citizens is the same. Imagine sitting in a symphony hall and being asked to vote on a succession of musical pieces. At first, there is little background noise, just the music being played. Over time, gradually, the volume of background noise increases until it is difficult to hear much of the music being played by the symphony. A personal television monitor appears at each seat, and people are able to turn to a video program of their choosing, including programs that focus on one section of the symphony. The challenge of voting for the best piece of symphony music has become far more difficult relative to the set of skills we would consider reasonable for the audience. This example illustrates my assertion that the behaviors required for effective citizenship in today's information environment are different than those required by past generations.

Another background theme we might pick up from today's information stream is that we cannot hold public officials accountable for fixing "the system." This accountability myth holds that our individual members of Congress are powerless to change a system that seems stuck between dysfunction and gridlock. But dysfunction and gridlock seem to result from many small, individual choices and actions. It is often easy to rationalize those choices and actions by their effect in optimizing short-term outcomes. The best solution to the larger problems of dysfunction and gridlock may be to hold officials responsible for their individual behaviors that feed the larger problem. Individual members of Congress are *not* powerless to solve the problems of gridlock and dysfunction. Everyone has a role to play in the solution. It likely is true that the solution is not implementation of some dramatically transformational law, policy or initiative. Elected officials are capable of doing their part to transform the system, and we can all help by establishing the right kind of specific behavioral accountability for the officials representing our district and our state.

The fourth background theme we might pick up from our information stream is what I call the complexity myth—the notion that the problems and issues we face today are so complex that they exceed the capacity of average citizens to resolve. There are many reasons for the information stream to project this theme. For one thing, journalists discussing any issue want to—or should want to—put that issue in context. Adding the broader context tends to make issues complex. Also, appealing to fear is a sound strategy for motivating an audience. We are psychologically predisposed to identifying and focusing on threats, then acting to protect ourselves from those threats. Complex problems, particularly those that seem to defy solution, are more likely to inspire fear than are problems with obvious solutions. So journalists increase the appeal of their work by accentuating the negative consequences of the issues they cover. A friend once told me that nothing gets attention in Washington except through hyperbole and exaggeration.

Solutions to complex problems frequently involve breaking the problem down into its constituent parts, then taking simple steps to solve the smaller component issues first. These simpler solutions may be easily conceived and implemented once we stop trying to craft overly complex solutions to resolve the larger issue. Engaging in dialogue with our elected officials, especially our representatives in Congress, is a great way to explore possible solutions to the problems we see around us. The availability of e-mail and web site communications, in addition to traditional correspondence via mail, make such dialogue more accessible than ever before. At the very least, exchanging our best ideas on solutions to social problems will allow us to better understand the challenges surrounding these problems.

The final myth—the polarization myth—tells us the problems we face have polarized our systems and citizens to the point that we can't agree on solutions. Again, part of the root cause of this theme lies in the commercialized information industry's competitive quest for viewers and readers. Conflict sells better than descriptive narratives of well-functioning processes.

In addition to the bias for conflict on the part of the media, the candidates who are often the subjects of political issue reporting are also striving to differentiate themselves in the eyes of the voters. One does not differentiate herself by noting similarities with the views of opposing politicians. Rather, both parties differentiate their value proposition by accentuating how they are different from the other party. Both the media industry covering political issues and the politicians who find themselves in the spotlight seek to highlight the differences in the views of opposing politicians. And the target of both the media and the candidate is often the relatively small groups of people who actually vote in political primaries and in non-presidential federal elections. The audience comprises people with political convictions strong enough to motivate above-average political participation. The views that resonate with this audience may well tend to reinforce a theme of polarization.

In fact, however, our political system is built upon compromise. The majority of voting-age Americans, the 63 percent who have not been voting in non-presidential federal elections, are likely to include those less passionate about specific solutions proposed by one end of the spectrum or the other. Tapping in to the power of this central block of voters would open up a range of compromise that seems inaccessible when we are listening only to either end of the spectrum.

There are features of our commercialized information industry that tend to infuse the information stream with themes likely to attract readers and viewers. These common themes may coalesce as the five myths I have described. But our psychology may also incline us to absorb these negative themes from the world around us. The five myths are basically ways we project blame on the world around us for the intractable problems we experience. Those problems, however, may be more a function of decreasing engagement with our government officials on the part of individual voters than with any systemic flaws in our government.

Psychologically, it is much easier for us to interpret the world through the lens of the five myths than to acknowledge our own personal accountability for much of what we experience. The book *Leadership and Self-Deception* explores the thesis that people tend to find it easier to blame others than to accept personal responsibility for the problems they experience. The book makes a convincing case that we all need great discipline and focus to overcome this natural tendency.[16] It is plausible that some of the appeal of the five myths lies in our own psychology rather than in the descriptive accuracy of the myths themselves.

In over thirty years as a leader in the military and in business, I have found that people tend to live up or down to the expectations we create for them. Our information environment tends to project the negative expectations I have labeled the five myths. If large numbers of us passively absorb these messages, then our failure to adapt to changes in the information environment might be interfering with our ability to effectively govern ourselves.

Committing ourselves to devote our limited time to learning about issues we have identified as our personal priorities shields us somewhat from passively absorbing priorities and messages projected by others. I call this active process of structuring the way we process information "being appropriately positive." Active consumers of information who apply reason and fairness in evaluating issues and trends empower themselves to see the world as it is rather than as we might see it through the lens of myths projected by the information stream.

Contributing Our Perspective and Transforming the Information Stream

Part of the positive structure we adopt as active consumers of information should be the practice of providing feedback to add our perspective to the information stream. Most newspapers, for example, allow readers to submit brief statements to an opinion section or letters to the editor. Many web

---

16 The Arbinger Institute, *Leadership and Self- Deception*, (San Francisco: The Arbinger Institute, 2010), 66–73.

sites offer a way for readers to post comments to a blog. Our members of Congress have web sites. Most invite correspondence by mail, e-mail, or web post. Today's information environment offers us more opportunities than ever before to participate in the social dialogue about the issues we face.

We are all better off when more citizens participate routinely and respectfully in these venues. For one thing, broader participation will tend to moderate the tone of debate over many issues, reducing the perception of polarization. Broader participation should bring out more ideas and possible solutions. A healthy dialogue may reveal whether there are simple solutions for problems that appear complex on the surface.

Our participation is also likely to help us discover where consensus lies, especially if we require our representatives to post the summary results of the input they receive for us to see. Most individual views will be shared by some number of other citizens who will be encouraged to offer their own views by positive example. We empower our members of Congress if we give them solid evidence of where the bulk of public opinion lies. Officials can act with confidence, knowing they are representing the views of those who elected them. In cases where the consensus view differs from the member's personal view, we open up the opportunity for dialogue.

Finally, making a habit of submitting letters to the editor or posting your opinion to a blog affirms the value of individual efforts to be active consumers of information and active participants in society. By adding our voices as individuals to the information stream, we provide value-rich content and help dilute special interest messaging. Many of us belong to groups or associations that represent one dimension of our lives. But it is our individual voice that blends the many dimensions of our lives as parents, patients, workers, and consumers of recreation and other public services. Absent this holistic perspective, the sterile voice of special interests assumes outsized proportions in the public dialogue.

A Guide To Appropriately Positive Behaviors

I have tried to explain that the concept of "being appropriately positive" is essentially the practice of adopting a positive structure for becoming an active consumer of information. Perhaps at this point, it would be useful to share one view of what this pattern of behavior might look like. Of course, there are many options for alternative individual structures that would achieve the desired end state.

One might begin by reviewing the political courage test on the Votesmart.org web site. The sixteen issues listed in alphabetical order in the 2012 Congressional edition of the test are abortion, Afghanistan, budget, campaign finance, capital punishment, economy, education, energy, environment, guns, health care, immigration, marriage, national security, social security, and spending/taxes. Once prioritized according to your individual values, you should ask yourself if there are any issues that should be on your list that are not on the political courage test list. If the answer is yes, then you should add those issues in the appropriate place on the list. You may find that some issues overlap in your mind, and that is fine. My way of dealing with that situation is to group those issues together in a rough priority order.

The next step is to identify the number of issues you are comfortable treating as your top priorities: these are the issues for which you make a personal commitment to actively engage the information stream. Specifically, the commitment to treat an issue as a top priority is a commitment to seek information from a range of sources over a period of weeks or months in order to form your personal, balanced and informed opinion on that priority issue. Many factors will affect the number of issues you identify as your top priorities. You should be open to changing the number of top priorities on your list as your work and family commitments change, for instance. I think a good general rule is to limit your top priorities to no more than three to five issues.

Appreciate the difficulty and importance of identifying and limiting your top priorities. Remember, there will be important issues that you will have to exclude from your list of top priorities because you simply do not have the time to treat every issue as a top priority. This is okay. Over time, you can reevaluate and change your top priorities. As you become knowledgeable about some issues, you will likely find that it takes less time to stay current on those issues, and this will make room for other important issues to make it on to your top priority list. But as a first step, you must give yourself a manageable list of top priorities. I would even go so far as to say it is probably better to limit your list too much than to create a list that is too long.

The next step is to set a schedule that allows you to study information about your top priority issues from a balanced range of sources over some reasonable period of time. You may decide to schedule time for one issue per day or one issue per week. You may determine that the time available for all of your top priority issues should be limited by your ability to read two articles about each of your top priority issues each week or each month. The specific technique you use to manage the process of learning about your top priority issues is largely a matter of personal preference. The key is to implement a consistent program that allows you to make steady progress in achieving a balanced, informed opinion about each of your top priority issues.

Remember to allow for time to survey a balanced range of sources for emerging issues and trends. This essential feature of your schedule ensures you do not miss some event that changes your priorities or introduces a new priority. Survey techniques include scanning the front page of one or more newspapers each day or one day each week. Allowing time for a survey technique keeps your routine fresh by adding variety to the time you devote to active learning about your priority issues.

As you begin your journey to being an active consumer of information, remember to take notes on your top priority issues. Observe any themes that emerge from your research. Compare your list to the themes I discussed earlier in this chapter. Question the soundness of these themes. Decide whether they are accurate descriptions of the world or merely convenient vehicles for packaging information in ways that increase readership and viewership.

Share your perspectives on your top priority issues with your elected representatives. Sharing your priorities and your views with your representative and understanding the views others have shared with your representative are essential steps to holding representatives accountable for their positions. Consider sharing your views in a letter to the editor or a blog to increase awareness and participation in the public dialogue.

Your respectful participation in the public dialogue about your top priority issues is important. It is important that the tone of your participation remain respectful and reasonable at all times. By example, you are likely to inspire others to share their views, and to adopt a similar tone. Your reasoning may change some people's minds on an issue or, at least, show them that there are sound reasons for positions other than their own. Either way, it is likely that more participation in public discussions of key issues will dilute the effect of special interest messaging and improve the degree to which the information stream reflects the true majority views and values of our country.

Your elected representatives should have an automated system for cataloguing and coding the input of the people they represent. Pay attention to the quality of this system. If you are forced to put your comment into a category that is not quite right, you should ask the representative and her staff to add an appropriate category.[17] This seems like a small point, but it is critical that your communications be put in the right categories. Elected representatives will likely see the aggregated number of comments on any particular category of issue as an indication of the need to act on that issue. Any inefficiency in category definitions will distort representatives' view of voter priorities and positions.

There is a standard debate in basic political science classes about whether representatives should simply act in accordance with the expressed preferences of the people who elected them or act in accordance with their personal judgment of what is best for the country. There is no doubt much room for disagreement on this point. But there should be no disagreement that the representative's job is to understand the preferences of the people who elected them. Even those who feel representatives should act on their personal judgment must agree that an accurate assessment of the views of the electorate should be an important input in forming the judgment of a representative on any issue. This is the essence of representative government.

We should insist on our representatives having an effective system for cataloguing the input of the people who elected them. In order to ensure that this system is effective, we should insist on public access to the summary data from this system. We should insist on periodic audits by impartial third party companies to validate the input and the summary made available for public view. Without public access to summary data describing constituent input, it is more difficult to hold representatives accountable for their positions on issues. If we know the aggregate of the input that representatives have received, we can compare that to the actual votes and behaviors of the representative. Representatives who have taken action inconsistent with voter preferences should acknowledge that fact and explain the reasons for their action. Understanding what our elected representatives have done and how that compares to the guidance they have received is essential to holding those representatives accountable for their actions.

---

17   I recently had this experience when I attempted to tell one of my senators that I disapproved of his failure to take Votesmart.org's political courage test. There was no appropriate category for such a complaint about the senator's performance. I wrote a separate e-mail and letter about this issue.

A standard elementary school exercise demonstrates to children how easily the process of communication can distort a message. The teacher takes one student into the hallway and gives that student a moderately detailed piece of information. Then the teacher goes back in the classroom and sends other students out to the hallway one at a time. The first student in the hallway verbally passes the message to the next student who comes out then the first student rejoins the class. After the message has been passed from one person to the next through the entire class, the last student comes in from the hall and writes the message they received on the board. The class then compares what the teacher told the first student with what the last student wrote on the board. Invariably, the message is significantly distorted by the communication process. Little inefficiencies in individual communication are compounded, often with dramatic effect.

Being appropriately positive means adopting a positive structure for being an active consumer of information. Any such positive structure for being an active consumer of information must include an effort to ensure that communication between voters and representatives are as concise and error-free as possible. Each of us must take responsibility for communicating our views to our elected representatives and for ensuring that our views are accurately received and catalogued by those representatives.

Being appropriately positive allows us to achieve and retain a reasonable view of the political system in the United States and the history of change within that system. No system is perfect, but ours is as effective as a human system can claim, based on history and scale. As passive consumers of an information stream shaped by special interests, we are led to dwell on the negative aspects of our history or current system; there are many. Becoming an active consumer of information is not a choice to ignore reality, but rather a choice to evaluate current issues and trends through the lens of your own vision and values.

THREE

Being Appropriately Informed

"Where, under our Declaration of Independence, does the Saxon man get his power to deprive all women and Negroes of their inalienable rights?"

—Susan B. Anthony

Accountable citizens are appropriately informed. Government acts for all of us at local, state, and federal level each day. Through a variety of taxes and fees, each of us helps pay for what government does. When we register our vehicles or pay for a driver's license or pay taxes on our food or pay our income taxes, we are contributing money to support government activities. When government at any level uses our money to act, it is reasonable to assume the government acts with our consent. Government is essentially a service we have hired to take care of certain things on our behalf. Accepting our responsibility for government action means that we accept accountability for what government does and does not do. Accepting accountability for actions we do not understand is at least unreasonable and probably negligent. Therefore, we should make an effort to be appropriately informed in order to exercise our citizenship in a reasonable, responsible way.

Being appropriately informed has more to do with applying basic time management and information management techniques than with one's level of education. Many highly educated people are not well informed. Some of the most well-informed people I know are high school graduates who have not had the time or opportunity to complete college. The choice to be well informed is a choice to apply reason to the flood of information that hits us from all directions each day. Basically, we must first choose what information we want to seek out and process. Using a little self discipline, the choice to be appropriately informed is a choice we can all make: the choice is to apply common-sense techniques over time to build and maintain a set of reasonable positions on issues that we consider important individually and collectively.

I intend this dimension of *Accountability Citizenship*—being appropriately informed—as a tool that empowers each of us to vote our individual values and beliefs. It should never be considered a filter for any eligible person to exclude herself or any other eligible person from the voting process. We can hope that many people will apply the lessons of this book and take advantage of the many sources of free information available. I especially hope that any who have avoided voting because they felt unable to defend their choice will take courage from this chapter. The implication of *The Wisdom of Crowds* is clear: we are more likely to reach a better collective decision when our elections include the individual, independent votes of a larger share of the electorate than when our elections include just the votes of some self-selected minority of the population.[18]

Basic Critical Reasoning

Voltaire said, "Common sense is not so common." Applying reason to our thoughts in a disciplined way is a learned skill, but most people never take the time to learn it. A number of simple, short guides are widely available, such as Anthony Weston's *A Rulebook for Arguments*. In this context, an "argument" is the conclusion you want to propose or evaluate, coupled with statements offered in support of that conclusion. It is not the contentious exchange of ideas most of us think about when we think of the common definition of an argument.

Applying reason to arguments is a process of evaluating the truth of the statements offered in support of a conclusion and then evaluating whether the statements together really do support the conclusion. Guides such as Weston's *Rulebook* provide clear, simple rules for using reason to develop your own

---

18   Surowiecki, *The Wisdom*, 57.

arguments as well as for evaluating the arguments of others.[19] I recommend finding a guide you are comfortable with using. Invest the time to read it and then refer to it periodically to keep from falling back into bad habits.

Once comfortable using reason to develop and evaluate arguments, you are ready to refine your list of social and political issues to help you reach the goal of being appropriately informed. As discussed in the last chapter, a list of social and political issues, in order of their importance to you, will allow you to prioritize the time you spend processing the flood of information that confronts all of us each day. It allows you to decide quickly which information you will accept for processing and which information you will deflect as irrelevant to your notion of what is important for our society and our country. The ability to focus your limited time on the issues you consider most important is essential to becoming appropriately informed on those issues. There is simply not enough time for each of us to be sufficiently informed on every issue that the world throws at us each day. The purpose of the list, therefore, is to allow each of us to become appropriately informed on issues that we consider most relevant to our role as a citizen.

The ability to use reason to develop and evaluate arguments is one tool that can help you to build, defend, and modify your personal list of high priority issues. Your list will almost certainly be different than my list, and that is okay. However, I do want to argue that there are some limits on what should make it on a reasonable list of social and political issues. There are also some minimal requirements for achieving the goal of being appropriately informed with regard to the issues on your list. The limits on a reasonable list of social and political issues come from the purpose of the list. For the list to be useful as a tool for citizen accountability, it should be a list of issues that some number of other citizens also consider important.

Certainly, there will be disagreement about what constitutes a reasonable list. Disagreement is fine. But remember, the tool is also an instrument for time management. If you insist on keeping things on your list that many or most other citizens do not consider important, then you will spend time learning about an issue that may never be relevant to the social and political choices you are asked to make. If most people agree that the essential elements of the top grade of apples are some combination of flavor, odor, and color, you can choose to insist that shape should also be on the list. No one will be able to make you take "shape" off your list. However, when you argue that a particular apple should be a top-grade apple because of its

---

19   Anthony Weston, *A Rulebook for Arguments*, 4th ed., 1–57

shape, your argument will not persuade those who believe flavor, odor, and color are more important characteristics. Your criterion will not be relevant to the group's decision-making process for selecting top-grade apples.

As you select and modify the issues for your list, you will rely on beliefs and values you have accumulated to this point in your life. To be truly informed on any issue, you should carefully and objectively consider the arguments against the conclusions you find most appealing. You should be open to reexamining your beliefs and values in light of the most current information available. In fact, one of the most important things we should all learn as we become more informed is that our knowledge has limits and constraints. The realization that your beliefs and values are not perfect should move you to be more tolerant of people with different beliefs and values.

I suspect many of you will resist the idea that cherished beliefs should be questioned. Whether we inherit these beliefs from those who nurture us in our youth or learn them by dint of experience, we acquire belief sets in deeply personal ways. The notion that each of us must reexamine our fundamental beliefs on a regular basis will make some uncomfortable. Conservative readers may view this idea as evidence that *Accountability Citizenship* is a liberal conspiracy; liberal readers may view it as evidence the book is a conservative plot. It is neither. But a major premise of *Accountability Citizenship* is that our views about the world and other people are all, necessarily, imperfect. The process of acknowledging this fact and striving to compensate for it should make us more tolerant and wise.

Remember that the generation that wrote our Declaration of Independence and Constitution were largely slaveholders. They explicitly set up a system that perpetuated the treatment of some human beings as property because of the color of their skin. They refused to give half of their number equal rights to vote and participate in society because of gender. We, collectively, sustained these prejudices for generations, even though some of our fellow citizens, from the earliest days of our republic, were pointing out the inconsistencies between these practices and the ideals expressed in our charters of government.

Now, certainly, many of you will have strong emotional reactions to the historical facts contained in the last paragraph. Some will want to argue that, given the social conventions prevalent around the world in the 18th century, it would have been impossible for the founding fathers to have done anything differently. But the facts are clear: over the past 237 years, we have revised the social definition of what it means to be a human being. The fact that we could disagree at any point in history on something so fundamental is strong evidence for the premise that we should be open to examining even our most cherished beliefs.

Thomas Sowell's *A Conflict of Visions* is the most elegant expression I have encountered of how intelligent people can reason to fundamentally different conclusions on the same issue. Sowell proposes that each of us reason from different "visions" of human nature. He presents two ends of the spectrum as the constrained vision and the unconstrained vision but is careful to note that each of us may apply different parts of the spectrum to various aspects of our set of values and beliefs. Basically, the constrained vision is the sense of human beings as being limited by our self-interest. On this view, people will behave selfishly by nature. Government must craft trade-offs and establish incentives for actions that are desirable for optimal social harmony. The unconstrained vision is the sense of human beings as capable of rising above self-interest to act for the greatest good of all. From this perspective, the role of government is to enable people to achieve their potential by eliminating incentives and trade-offs that encourage constrained behavior. Reasoning from different starting points on the spectrum of visions leads reasonable people to different conclusions.[20]

Sowell's work allowed me to acknowledge the rationality of others' views without giving in to the popular temptation to demonize those with different beliefs and values as evil or stupid or selfish. Sowell's distinction is not a cure for political and social disagreement, but I believe it offers a path to restore a higher level of civility in our discourse. It may be the case that seemingly intractable problems can be advanced or resolved by leaders willing to discuss solutions and compromises without the emotional handcuffs of strict partisan ideology.

Being appropriately informed requires an attempt to understand the rationality of opposing views. The attempt to understand opposing views grants a basic human dignity to the people who believe in those views even though we may continue to disagree. If there is one lesson to be taken from our history, it is that the prevailing sentiment on even the most basic issues may still be wrong. How else can we explain the difference between the concept of equality as expressed in our Declaration of Independence and the history of slavery and discrimination in America? The key to resolving even the most vexing problems we face is to acknowledge the dignity and worth of the people who espouse a different point of view from our own.

---

20 Thomas Sowell, *A Conflict of Visions* (New York: William Morrow and Co., 1987), 1–39.

A Practical Example: Honest Doublespeak and Our Federal Budget[21]

Government officials measure and report on the federal budget using different baselines and techniques that can create honest confusion about the effect of a proposed policy or proposal. Two distinct agencies provide budget estimates: the Office of Management and Budget (OMB) provides budget analysis for the president, and the Congressional Budget Office (CBO) provides analysis for Congress. Each agency uses something called a baseline, which projects the current level of spending into the future. Each baseline incorporates assumptions about inflation and other economic variables. OMB's baseline, also known as current service estimates, covers five years while CBO's baseline budget projections cover ten years. Policy, budget proposals, and legislation are "scored" in reference to one or the other baseline. The normal procedure assigns a score based on the impact of the policy, proposal, or legislation over the full period of the baseline used.

Understanding the context for any statement about the cost or the savings associated with a particular policy or proposal is essential. For one thing, the magnitude of any increase or savings will vary according to the baseline used. More importantly, however, the same proposal can be truthfully described as a program cut or as sustaining current levels of spending depending on whether the point of reference is one of the baselines or the current spending level. In *The Federal Budget: Politics, Policy, Process*, Allen Schick offers an example of a baseline that shows a $41 million increase over five years. A hypothetical policy to cap inflation increases and other variables reduces the increase to $22 million. Schick points out that an official could refer to this hypothetical policy as increasing spending by $22 million (over current levels) or as cutting spending by $19 million over five years (from the baseline projection).[22]

It is important to understand that there is no standard for a single right way to describe a policy or proposal. Officials are free to use whatever standard they deem appropriate. It is not dishonest or shady for politicians on opposite sides of an issue to use the reference that best supports their position. Assuming most elected officials are passionately committed to

---

21 The facts and examples in this section are taken from Allen Schick, *The Federal Budget: Politics, Policy, Process,* 3rd ed. (Washington: Brookings Institution Press, 2007), 62–70.
22 Ibid., 67–8.

doing what they believe is best for our country, I would expect them to use the numbers that portray proposals they support in the most favorable light. However, voters deserve an "apples to apples" comparison of any given proposal, so we can make the best choice for ourselves about whether to support or oppose that proposal. We will not get that clear standard unless we engage our elected officials and demand it.

Requiring a clear statement of the impact of any proposed policy or legislation with reference to both baselines and to current spending levels would resolve much of the confusion about controversial issues facing our country. Imagine politician A arguing that we should support a policy because it will have a certain budget impact X. Now another politician B confronts A, and tells us the policy is a bad policy because it has budget impact Z. Without knowing the basis for the budget impact numbers in this discussion, we are left to conclude that one of the politicians is ignorant or dishonest. Once we insist that both politicians frame their discussion by stating the budget impact is X (with regard to the CBO baseline), Y (with regard to current spending), and Z (with regard to the OMB baseline), we transform the discussion. We no longer have to conclude that one of the politicians is ignorant or dishonest. We can see that each politician is using different assumptions to support their position. Furthermore, we can choose between positions based on the assumptions we consider most relevant. I believe we should require all elected officials to use three points of reference—CBO, OMB, and current spending level—whenever they cite budget impacts in support or opposition of a policy or proposal.

Accountability Citizenship and the History of the United States

Beyond the basic tools for applying reason to filter and evaluate issues and candidates, there is some fundamental information about the history of our republic that is important to being appropriately informed. Much of the history of America is the struggle for internal equality and fairness: a quest to establish in law and to honor in practice the fundamental dignity of all persons. We have also struggled imperfectly to create and abide by the same standard for people of other nations. The actions which best reflect our founding principles have often been in conflict with more powerful commercial and practical interests. Our history indicates that without the informed and peaceful engagement of a majority of citizens, we cannot assume the political processes of the United States will produce outcomes consistent with our most basic values.

The version of United States' history that most of us learn in school should be just a starting point for a lifelong process of learning about our past. The most valuable outcome of such a starting point should be the realization that our successes and failures as a nation are a function of the actions or inaction of the people of the United States. Clinging to a romanticized account of our past not only fails to achieve this outcome, but it also creates mistrust and cynicism as individuals confront alternative sources and achieve new insights.

What follows is a short survey of the history of the United States. As you will see, it springs from many sources. While I attempt to stick closely to facts, the selection of facts itself is a subjective endeavor and many of you will disagree with my selection. I have chosen to touch on founding principles, on slavery and women's suffrage, and on early expansion and foreign policy. I believe these chapters show that we have failed to live up to our founding principles in many ways, but that we are capable of living up to these principles. To avoid repeating the mistakes of the past, I believe we must each participate in shaping the vision and values of our republic by focusing on the behaviors and performance of the officials we elect to represent us, especially those in Congress.

Remember, the purpose of this narrative is to inform my engagement with my elected officials. You can choose an alternative narrative to inform your engagement. Just as with your list of priorities, reason constrains the narrative you choose. If you choose a narrative that is not tied to generally accepted facts, your framework will not support effective engagement with your elected officials.

A Brief and Selective History of the Early United States

Our republic is founded on a Constitution. That Constitution was developed after a group of dissatisfied colonists—subjects of the British Empire—declared their independence from Great Britain and fought a war to win their independence at great risk to themselves and to their families. The colonists were dissatisfied because they believed the British government was abusing its power, treating them unjustly, and not responding to their needs. The first effort to structure a unified government for the new United

States was based on something known as the Articles of Confederation, and it was a failure. Generally, historians agree the Articles of Confederation did not provide the central government with sufficient powers to administer the basic functions of a viable government. The Constitution was developed in 1787 to address the shortcomings of the Articles of Confederation. The Constitution is not perfect either—it has been amended twenty-seven times. The first ten amendments were adopted in 1791 and are known collectively as the Bill of Rights.

Seventy-four years after the Constitution was formally approved, we suffered four terrible years of Civil War because we could not agree on the issues of slavery and the relative powers of the state and federal governments. From 1861 to 1865, the Civil War claimed the lives of approximately six hundred and twenty-five thousand Americans. Abraham Lincoln's 1860 election on a Republican platform that included a pledge to keep slavery out of the western territories prompted the secession of several southern states. South Carolina seceded from the Union in December of 1860, followed by Mississippi, Alabama, Georgia, Florida, and Louisiana in January 1861. State militias in South Carolina, Georgia, Alabama, and Florida seized federal installations, arsenals, and armories in January 1861. The federal government refused to recognize the legitimacy of secession even as other states seceded and joined the Confederate States of America. By the time Abraham Lincoln was inaugurated on March 4, Texas had also seceded and seized the federal arsenal at San Antonio. Confederate forces opened fire on Fort Sumter on April 12 and captured the fort on April 13. Lincoln responded with a blockade and a call for volunteers. The federal army eventually conquered and occupied the Confederate states. In April 1865, Lincoln was assassinated; Confederate military forces surrendered across the south and an armistice was signed. The Thirteenth Amendment ending slavery was adopted as part of the Constitution in December of 1865.

But the end of the war and the adoption of the Thirteenth Amendment did not solve the problems of discrimination, human dignity, and civil rights. For over one hundred years after the end of the Civil War, African Americans and other minorities fought domestic terrorism, harassment, and discrimination. The Fourteenth and Fifteenth Amendments ostensibly gave African Americans and other minorities the rights of citizenship and the ability to vote, but in practice these rights were systematically denied in many parts of the country. The passage of the Civil Rights Act in 1964 marked a significant milestone in the struggle for equality. The peaceful persistence of people like Dr. Martin Luther King and Cesar Chavez raised awareness of shortcomings in law and in behaviors. A series of important decisions by the courts have supported and strengthened the law.

Besides the struggle of African American and other racial minorities, women also struggled against inequality from the earliest days of our republic. In fact, it wasn't until the Twenty-Second Amendment was ratified in 1920 that women were given the right to vote. The path to the Twenty-Second Amendment was long and arduous. Women leaders such as Lucy Stone, Elizabeth Cady Stanton, Susan B. Anthony, and Alice Paul led a peaceful movement for change and persisted in the face of ridicule, harassment, imprisonment, and brutal treatment. Legislation prohibiting discrimination on the basis of gender and providing penalties for sexual harassment have greatly improved conditions, but behaviors undermining equality persist.[23]

The expansion of the United States westward across the continent came by seizing lands originally occupied by Native Americans. The campaigns to subdue these tribes were brutal. Both sides committed atrocities. The United States government broke treaty after treaty with Native American tribes. In the aftermath of the wars and forced migrations, the government generally failed to provide adequately for the people we had conquered and displaced.[24] Our Native American peoples have had their own unique struggle to address the legacy of this period and to gain their civil rights.

The United States was not the first nation to lay claim to much of the territory we occupied in our march westward. During our colonial period, France had claimed much of the interior lands west of the Mississippi. Spain had claimed the area now covered by the states of Florida, Texas, New Mexico, Arizona, California, Nevada, Utah and Colorado. Russia held what is now Alaska. The United States purchased the territorial rights claimed by France in the Louisiana Purchase of 1803, effectively doubling the size of the country at that time. In 1819, the United States purchased the rights claimed by Spain in Florida. Two years later, Mexico won its independence from Spain. Under the Treaty of Cordoba, Mexico assumed sovereignty of all territories previously claimed by Spain in the American southwest. In 1824, a dictator suspended the Mexican Constitution and rebellions erupted in several places in Mexico. Texas gained its independence from Mexico in 1836, existing as an independent republic until it was annexed by the United

---

23 Jean Baker, *Sisters: The Lives of America's Suffragists* (New York: Hill and Wang, 2005).

24 Zinn, *A People's History*, 125–148.

States in 1845. The United States fought a war with Mexico from 1846 to 1848. The Treaty of Guadalupe Hidalgo ended the war in 1848 with the United States paying Mexico $18 million and taking control of all territory north and west of the Rio Grande including California. In 1867, the United States purchased Alaska from the Russians for $7.2 million. The Kingdom of Hawaii was overthrown by American and European businessmen in 1893. The United States annexed Hawaii in July of 1898 despite the opposition of a majority of native Hawaiians. Both Alaska and Hawaii remained territories until 1959 when they became the 49th and 50th states respectively.

An unvarnished view of the history of the United States forces us to confront many unpleasant facts. In our treatment of citizens as well as others subject to our laws and powers, the people of the United States have frequently acted no better than the people of other nations, and our government no better than other governments. The founding principles of our country were a unique expression of individual dignity and liberty in 1776, but our 237-year struggle to realize in practice the ideas implied by these founding principles teach us that we cannot accept a romanticized view of our republic at face value. The words of the Declaration of Independence and Constitution are only as good as the sum of our individual efforts to make the policies and practices of our government conform to the spirit of those words.

Accountability citizenship requires that each of us accept responsibility and accountability for all that our country does or fails to do. It is not enough to blame dysfunctional government as if it were a thing apart: our government is designed to be of the people, by the people, and for the people. Even when we disagree with the chosen course, we are responsible and accountable for registering that disagreement with our votes and with our persistent and peaceful engagement with elected officials.

Who Can Vote?

In general, anyone who is a citizen of the United States and over eighteen years of age can vote.[25] People must register to vote in accordance with the

---

25 People who have been declared mentally incompetent are not eligible to vote. People convicted of felonies are not eligible to vote while they are serving time in prison. After being released from prison, convicted felons regain their right to vote.

laws of their state[26] and generally must be able to prove they are citizens in order to register. The purpose of voter registration and voter identification requirements is to prevent election fraud. Specifically, the idea is that voters must be registered to ensure people do not vote in more than one place or cast more than one vote during a single election. It is against the law to falsely claim to be a citizen in order to register to vote.

Federal law requires citizens to show proof of identity when they register by mail to vote for the first time. Many states require proof of identity at the time an individual appears to vote. According to the Election Assistance Commission (EAC), proof of identity includes a current form of photo identification or a current utility bill, bank statement, government check, paycheck, or government document showing name and address.

Voter registration forms may have a space for an address, but even people who have no address are supposed to be able to vote as long as they have proof of identification. The federal form for voter registration, which may be used to register in any state, includes a space where a citizen may draw a map showing where they live. Therefore, even homeless citizens should be able to register to vote.

Regardless of where you are physically located at the time of the election, absentee voting procedures allow you to register and to vote. Citizens living outside the United States can get a federal postcard application on military bases or at the American embassy or consular offices. The EAC provides information and assistance to citizens to streamline the voter registration process for all fifty states and to serve as a single source of information for nearly any situation.[27]

The right to vote is one of the most fundamental rights of citizenship in our republic. During much of the history of the United States, groups of people were denied the right to vote because of the color of their skin or because of their gender. Sometimes, domestic terrorist groups such as the Ku Klux Klan used physical violence or the threat of physical violence to deny target groups the right to vote. Often, the right to vote was denied using passive techniques like a literacy requirement or a voting fee (poll tax) that affected some groups disproportionately. Although voters must register in accordance with the laws of their state, states may not include registration

---

26 All states except North Dakota require voters to register to vote. Wyoming does not allow voters to register by mail.

27 Election Assistance Commission Web site, http://www.eac.gov/voter_resources/register_to_vote.aspx

requirements that effectively deny the right to vote to any individual citizen or group of citizens.

We can say we have a representative form of government only if there is an effective mechanism for people to vote. Throughout our history, people have made great sacrifices to ensure all citizens have the right to vote. We should consider it our duty as citizens both to vote ourselves and to protect the right to vote for other citizens.

A Job Description for Our Members of Congress

Being appropriately informed includes understanding what our elected officials are supposed to do. We can deduce a reasonable job description from the documents that set the framework of our government. A number of resources make acquiring these useful documents quite easy: the government printing office distributes free copies of the Constitution and Declaration of Independence in an informative pamphlet that can be found in most public libraries. On the Internet, both the Constitution and Declaration of Independence are available for review.[28] The Votesmart.org web site also has a tab dedicated to "Government 101" that provides a nice overview of our government.[29] Taking advantage of available information is important to forming a general concept of what we should expect from our members of Congress. Such an understanding allows us to develop a job description for members of Congress, such as that shown in figure 3 below. Having a general job description for these public officials allows us to use basic performance management techniques to evaluate the performance of individual members of Congress—one of the key aspects of being appropriately engaged.

As stated in the preamble, the purpose of the Constitution is to "form a more perfect Union, establish Justice, insure domestic Tranquility, provide for the common defence, promote the general Welfare, and secure the Blessings of Liberty..."[30] It gives Congress exclusive power to pass laws to achieve its purpose. All proposed laws passed by Congress must be submitted to the president for approval. Even if a president vetoes a law,

---

28 View both the Declaration and the Constitution online at http://publications.usa. gov/USAPubs.php?PubID=1331.
29 "Government 101: Introduction," Votesmart.org, http://votesmart.org/education/government
30 U.S. Constitution, p. 9.

however, Congress can still enact it with the approval of two-thirds of both the House and the Senate. Furthermore, perhaps remembering one of the key grievances that led the colonists to start the Revolutionary War—taxation without representation—the framers of the Constitution specified that all bills for raising revenue originate in the House of Representatives and that no public money could be spent except as a consequence of a law passed by Congress.

In the Declaration of Independence, Thomas Jefferson wrote that governments derive their powers from the consent of the governed. From this philosophy and from the framework for our government established in the Constitution, we can deduce that the primary functions of a member of Congress are to learn what the people want and need; to propose, evaluate, and act on government measures to satisfy the people's wants and needs; and to confirm that the people agree with the member's proposals and evaluations. This is what it means for a member of Congress to represent the people from her district or state.

Members' votes should generally reflect the guidance received from the voters unless there is a good reason for a member to deviate from what the voters have requested. One can imagine circumstances in which a member of Congress has information that is either not available or not adequately understood by the general public. Certainly, in cases where the last guidance received from voters is contrary to what the member of Congress believes is best for the country, then the member should follow the course he believes is best for the country. But it is reasonable to expect such circumstances to be the exception rather than the rule. And it is reasonable to expect a member of Congress to be able to explain such circumstances at some point. In a republic where elected officials are supposed to represent us, the general rule should be that members of Congress act in accordance with the wishes of the voters they represent.

Each member of Congress receives thousands of letters and e-mails from constituents. They have staff and information systems, paid for with tax dollars, for processing and categorizing this correspondence. Each member of Congress has a web site. A reasonable expectation based on this sizeable taxpayer investment is that each of us should be able to see an anonymous summary of the issues raised by our fellow citizens. This summary should allow us to see the volume of correspondence and the relative weight of opinions received on each issue.

Besides establishing and maintaining a method for clearly communicating with voters, each member of Congress should be present for congressional deliberations and votes. We should ask our members to publish the total days of congressional deliberations and the number of days the member has missed. We should have the same data for members regarding their participation in the various committees to which they are assigned. Certainly, there are reasons for all of us to miss a day of work every now and then. However, we have a right to expect our public servants to hold themselves to a high standard in this area. Vacations and other personal time should be scheduled during the periods when Congress is not in session when possible. While perfect attendance may not be the most important metric for evaluating a member of Congress, it is reasonable to expect our public servants to be present for duty.

We should expect members of Congress to be honest, to be present for duty, and to generally carry out the wishes of the voters who elected them. In addition, however, voters can and should identify specific legislative actions they desire in order to address their highest-priority issues. It is reasonable for voters who make such requests to consider carrying out the requests to be part of the job description for their member of Congress. Such requests may be as simple as supporting a request for action by some government agency. They might be as complex as drafting, sponsoring, co-sponsoring, or opposing a specific piece of legislation. Of course, members will not be able to carry out all such requests because some requests will conflict. Certainly, in these cases, we should expect our members of Congress to decide how to act based on their own best judgment and the majority opinion of the voters they represent.

Besides knowing what members of Congress should do, being well-informed requires we must also know where and how to find out what our members of Congress actually have done. "Thomas" at the Library of Congress web site (http://thomas.loc.gov/home/thomas.php) provides information on both the House of Representatives and the Senate. One can research specific legislation and visit the web sites for individual members of Congress at the web sites for the United States House of Representatives (http://www.house.gov) and the United States Senate (http://www.senate. gov). Member voting records are available at the Votesmart.org web site (http://www.votesmart.org). This site also features a political courage test. Project Vote Smart asks members to take this test prior to each election. Regardless of whether members take the test voluntarily, Votesmart. org provides member-specific information. This information makes it possible for each of us to tailor a performance management scorecard for the representative and senators that represent us in Congress, and then evaluate how well individual members of Congress have carried out the tasks identified on the scorecard.

The preceding discussion establishes some reasonable guidelines for a basic job description for a member of Congress. You may develop a different job description based on the expectations you have for the members of Congress who represent you. The point is not developing a single job description: we can have different expectations. We can expect that members will win elections based on how well they fulfill the expectations of the majority of their constituents. The most important thing about our job description for our members of Congress is that it allows us to evaluate the individual performance of our members. We do not have to hold members of Congress accountable for all that the House or the Senate does. We can request that members of Congress comply with our general expectations for public servants and that they achieve specific, measurable objectives within their power as individuals. We can then hold them accountable for their success relative to this job description. This level of accountability is no different than the standard most of us live with at our daily jobs: we are measured on how well we comply with general expectations and achieve specific objectives assigned to us.

Figure 3: A Basic Job Description for Members of Congress

• Perform basic functions expected of all public servants.
  • Support and defend the Constitution of the United States.
  • Be honest and put the interests of the country first.
  • Be present for all required sessions, hearings, meetings and votes.
  • Be a good steward of the power vested in you by those you represent.
• Maintain effective two-way communications with those you represent.
  • Take the Political Courage test on votesmart.org .
  • Catalog and tabulate all correspondence from those you represent.
  • Display a current summary of all correspondence to show relative priorities.
  • Have summary and catalog audited regularly by impartial party.
  • Report results of audit and status of any corrective action required.
• Act effectively to achieve the legislative objectives of those you represent.
  • Display your priorities.
  • Explain differences between your priorities and constituent summary priorities.
  • Propose or co-sponsor legislation to achieve priorities.
  • Oppose measures that work against achieving priorities.
  • Clearly report the results of your actions.

Accountable citizens are appropriately informed. Being appropriately informed means having a basic grasp of critical reasoning, our government and our history, current events, and the basic roles of those we have elected. It means having a well-formed opinion on the most important issues facing our republic. It means researching those issues deemed most important by understanding the positions of those who think differently than we do and seeking a balance in the type of news we consume. Together, these skills and practices give individual citizens all they need to establish a performance management scorecard for each elected official that represents them. Building and maintaining such a scorecard is the subject of the next chapter—being appropriately engaged.

FOUR

Being Appropriately Engaged

"The basis of our political systems is the right of the people to make and to alter their Constitutions of Government. But the Constitution which at any time exists, 'till changed by an explicit and authentic act of the whole People is sacredly obligatory upon all."

— *George Washington, 1796*

Our Declaration of Independence states that all people have certain natural rights and that governments exist to secure those rights. But there is an inherent tension between the notion that we are all equally endowed with natural rights and the role of a government to secure them. After all, sooner or later, people exercising their rights to liberty and the pursuit of happiness are certain to come in conflict with others exercising the same rights in the same society. And government, according to the Declaration, exists to secure the rights of all citizens. Government can only secure the maximum liberty for all of us by creating boundaries that limit the right to liberty for each of us.

Because of the controversy associated with mediating between the rights of one and the rights of all, each of us should stay engaged and lend our voice to guide the process. No rights are absolute. The right to freedom of religion, for instance, does not extend so far as to allow for religions that call for human sacrifice. Other rights have boundaries as well. The right to free speech, for instance, may be used to justify unlimited campaign donations;

but one could argue that at some point, one person's unlimited contribution effectively deprives some less wealthy person of his right to free speech. At least, as the classic example goes, one's right to free speech does not extend so far as to cover the right to yell "Fire!" in a crowded theater. The government's mechanisms for mediating appropriate boundaries—impartial institutions such as courts and legislatures—depend on appropriate engagement by individual citizens.

When we collectivize our natural rights and empower a government to secure those rights with respect to other peoples and governments, the inevitable conflict is even more problematic because, in the international arena, there is not necessarily an impartial arbiter acknowledged by both parties. In such circumstances, it is easy for governments to create conflict and war by pursuing that for which governments exist—to secure the natural rights of citizens. Appropriate engagement on the part of all citizens is essential to ensuring governments exhaust all peaceful avenues of conflict resolution before resorting to force.

The government of the United States serves as our collective voice and agent by proxy. This is what it means to say we have a government of the people, by the people, and for the people. But collective entities by themselves—be they associations or corporations or governments—have no conscience. Conscience—the little voice inside each of us that tells us what we should do to be true to our values—is a function of our individual existence as human beings. The only way to ensure a group of any type acts with conscience is for the individuals who make up the group to actively shape the collective decision-making processes that drive the group's choices and actions.

We know from our brief survey of American history in the last chapter that the United States government is as capable of wrong-doing as any other government. In such a context, the only way to absolve oneself of responsibility for the wrongful acts of any government is to be appropriately engaged in that government's collective decision-making processes. Being appropriately engaged means that we vote at every opportunity, and that we communicate our vision and values to our elected officials as often as we can.

Congress is designed to be the most responsive engine for citizen engagement with our government. Each one of the 435 representatives in the House of Representatives stands for reelection every two years. One-third of the one hundred members of the United States Senate also stand for reelection every two years. The Constitution gives us the power to change 468 of the 535 members—87 percent of the United States Congress—every two years. The fact that the Constitution gives us the power to change members with such frequency is strong evidence that the people who designed our government intended Congress as the main channel by which the will of the people was projected into our government.

In this chapter, we will develop a scorecard to help you evaluate the performance of your members of Congress. Using a scorecard and basic performance management techniques is a great way to build confidence in your opinions and in your ability to communicate those opinions to others. But the ultimate measure of appropriate engagement is whether or not a citizen votes, and, in particular, whether that vote is in accordance with reasoned conclusions.

Engagement and Voting

The first and most important task to be appropriately engaged is to vote. No matter what else one does, it is the act of voting in accordance with one's individual vision and values that is most likely to improve the outcome of our collective decision-making processes. Even in the event that one is unable to complete the preparatory tasks outlined in the chapters on being appropriately positive and appropriately informed, voting remains the primary and most important duty of every citizen.

In fact, the entire structure of *Accountability Citizenship* is built to support increased voter participation. At the outset, we examined the question of why more people don't vote, and especially, why more people don't vote in non-presidential election years. I constructed the elements of *Accountability Citizenship*—being appropriately positive, appropriately informed, and appropriately engaged—to address the most likely reasons for non-voting behavior.

Primarily, I believe many people don't vote because they think their vote doesn't matter. I believe this is largely due to the perceived power of special interests. Just as George Washington did, I include political parties in the definition of "special interests."[31] Special interests have power because they control the money that politicians need to be reelected. Politicians need money to fund advertising. Political advertising is currently aimed at making candidates appealing to the people most likely to vote. A number of long-term trends, such as redistricting along party lines, tend to favor

---

31 Washington, "Farewell Address."

entrenched party interests. If we increase the number of Americans who vote regularly in federal elections, and we change the way those voters engage their representatives, we can shift the focus from special interest dollars to direct engagement with citizens. We can reestablish the practical requirement for elected officials to satisfy the demands of their constituents rather than simply do what political party leaders want.

Consider this example: a majority of elected officials have refused to take the nonpartisan political courage test sponsored by Votesmart.org. The political courage test requires officials to clearly record their positions on a number of important current issues. According to Votesmart.org, only 38 percent of officials took the test during the 2010 election cycle. When you look at the reasons our elected officials gave for not taking the test, some of which have been posted on Votesmart.org, you find that some claim leaders in both political parties discourage officials from providing answers to the test.[32] The number of members of Congress who chose not to take the political courage test in 2010 is a powerful example of how our elected representatives follow party guidance rather than doing what their constituents want them to do. In my view, every one of us should write letters to each of our elected federal officials and advise them that we want them to take the political courage test. A sample letter, similar to the one I sent to the members of Congress who represent me, is included in appendix A of this book.

Another reason people think their vote doesn't matter is because, as passive consumers of the information stream, they have absorbed the five myths discussed in chapter two. The techniques described under the headings of being appropriately positive and being appropriately informed should encourage people to make an active assessment of whether these myths are more false than true. The problem with passively accepting the myths is that they project a strongly negative view of the state of our society and of our ability to change it. We live in a country where the people can change government officials, policies, and programs. To the extent that we accept the truth of the myths, we concede that our country's political system is not working the way it is supposed to work. One could infer from *The Wisdom of Crowds* that a loss of faith in the basic fairness of our public institutions might undermine people's willingness to engage in cooperative behaviors such as payment of taxes and voting.[33] In turn, the effects of

32 Political Courage Test, Votesmart.org, http://www.votesmart.org/about/political-courage-test.pdf
33 Surowiecki, *The Wisdom*, 139.

reduced voting and payment of taxes may reinforce or create the situations that the myths describe.

Another major reason why people may not vote is that they do not feel confident either in their ability to make a good choice or in their ability to discuss and defend their choice. In this case, it is easier for people to come up with some excuse as to why they did not vote at all than it is for them to vote. I hope that the information about critical reasoning in chapter three will encourage at least some of the people who feel this way to become active voters.

Many of us are busy with our work and caring for our families. Preparing to vote can seem overwhelming at times. However, chapters 2 and 3 provide resources and techniques that would give this potentially overwhelming task some very simple and concrete dimensions. Writing down the issues that are most important to us as individuals and taking a few minutes each day to read a newspaper or peruse a free web site such as Votesmart.org are manageable techniques to support good voting behavior.

As I have noted as several points in this book, encouraging as many people as possible to vote using their individual vision, values, and perspective is far more important than the level of preparation of any individual voter. In other words, even if you cannot prepare at all, it is better for all of us collectively if you make time to vote in accordance with your individual sense of what is right. According to Surowiecki, the collective decision we reach will likely be better as we increase the diversity and independence of the voting population.[34]

One cautionary note in this regard: it is important for individuals to vote based on their own beliefs and values rather than in response to the reporting on the way an election seems to be trending. Following reported trends rather than one's personal convictions can lead a group decision process astray by creating what Surowiecki calls an information cascade. In a cascade, when people start following each other based on the assumption that the crowd is more likely right than wrong, the pattern of errors all tend to skew the group decision process in the same direction, increasing the error in the group outcome. When people vote based on their individual information, on the other hand, individual errors tend to cancel one another rather than reinforce one another; so the collective outcome is better overall. Since our information stream tends to report election results and forecast winners as each precinct and state complete their elections, there is a possibility that

---

34 Ibid., 57.

people in states where the polls close later will be influenced by projected outcomes from states that finished earlier. It is possible for this to occur in such a way as to create an information cascade.[35]

Voting and Scorecards: Performance Management for Elected Officials

As children in primary and secondary school, we were accustomed to being evaluated periodically based on how well we had mastered some body of knowledge or how well we had performed assigned tasks. Getting our report card was a stressful event for many of us. Transitioning to our adult lives, many of us find ourselves evaluated by those with whom we work using some form of performance management system. Performance management systems translate strategic objectives into individual tasks and projects, assign responsibility for those tasks and projects, and evaluate the performance of individuals who execute the tasks and projects. These systems are essential for any organization with more than a handful of employees to understand whether employees are meeting basic standards and to measure individual performance relative to group goals.

Performance management is conceptually simple: it is the set of processes and systems we use to *communicate* objectives and expectations for individuals and groups, coupled with processes and systems to *evaluate* performance within the established context. I prefer systems that communicate expected general behaviors and group norms (such as honesty and respect for coworkers) as well as specific, individually tailored objectives tied to group strategic goals. I am convinced that each of us should follow an individual performance management methodology for our elected federal officials, especially our members of Congress; and I want to offer a simple vision for what that might look like. A simple scorecard for our elected federal officials can be a useful way to increase voter confidence and participation.

When I assumed responsibility for human capital management at Overstock.com, one of the first systems I revised was the performance management system. At the time, the company was growing rapidly. We had an annual, paper-based performance appraisal system, and compliance varied across different departments. Over the course of several months, I

---

35 Ibid., 53–63.

formed a committee that developed and tested an automated performance appraisal system. By the end of the first year, everyone was trained on the new system, compliance was well above 90 percent, and we had a source of performance data we could use to measure the relative contributions of our associates. Putting a basic performance management system in place is easy as long as we don't over-complicate the requirements.

In the last chapter, I proposed a basic, generic job description for members of Congress. We can use this job description to build a scorecard for expected general behaviors. For instance, we probably all expect our members of Congress to be honest and to be present when Congress is in session. These elements of the scorecard are fairly clear. Other common elements may be less clear. For instance, we should all expect our members of Congress to fulfill their oath to support and defend the Constitution; however, it is certain that many of us will disagree about the specific behaviors that support and defend the Constitution.

Likewise, part of our performance management scorecard for elected representatives should reflect how well those representatives have accomplished tasks on our individual list of priority issues. And our individual lists of priority issues may be quite different from those of other voters. For instance, if my top priority issue was improving communication from members of Congress to their constituents, I may have written a letter[36] to members of Congress representing my district and state, advising them that I wanted the following specific behaviors to support this priority: (1) the member of Congress completes the political courage test sponsored by Votesmart.org; (2) The member of Congress posts a summary of constituent correspondence received by the member of Congress on the member's web site and updates it quarterly; and (3) the member posts her own scorecard of her performance to date reflecting the general behaviors for which she feels accountable along with individual achievements relative to her key priorities.

I would capture the priority "Improving communication with constituents" on my scorecard for each member of Congress for whom I am eligible to vote. I would score each of my members of Congress based on whether they had performed the specific behaviors I requested of them.

Let's say another of my top priorities was balancing the federal budget. I may have written a letter[37] to members of Congress representing my district and state, advising them that I wanted the following specific behaviors

---

36 See appendix A.
37 See appendix A.

to support this priority: (1) do not vote for any budget that calls for more spending in a given year than the government collects in revenue, (2) do not vote for any legislation to which measures have been added to authorize or appropriate funding for nonrelated activities or projects, and (3) report the budgetary effect of all legislation using the three reference points of current spending, Congressional Budget Office baseline and Office of Management and Budget baseline. I should add these specific items to my scorecard, and I should evaluate each of my representatives on how well they complied with these specific items.

Note that in these examples, I am not trying to hold individuals responsible for the behavior of Congress overall. Rather, I am holding the members of Congress for whom I vote accountable for whether or not they have carried out specific behaviors I asked them to carry out. Many performance management systems advocate using objectives that have certain characteristics. Useful performance objectives should be specific, measurable, achievable, realistic and timely. It is not realistic or achievable to try to hold an individual member of Congress accountable for the behavior of Congress as a whole. However, it is perfectly realistic and achievable for individual members of Congress to carry out specific behaviors like the ones in the examples above. If each of us insisted on specific behaviors, used scorecards to measure compliance with requested behaviors, and voted based on our evaluation, I believe we could rapidly make constituent satisfaction the main driver of Congressional activity.

Figure 4: Sample Scorecard for Members of Congress

Performance Criterion	Score (n =1-10)
Would you vote for this Member of Congress if the election was today?	n
Honesty	n
Puts Country Ahead of Party	n
Present for Duty	n
Good Steward	n
Took Votesmart.org Political Courage Test	n
Display/update summary of constituent priorities and correspondence on their website	n
Report budget impact of all legislation using three points of reference (current spending; CBO; OMB)	n
(Fill in the blank) Your legislative priority #1	n
(Fill in the blank) Your legislative priority #2	n

A sample scorecard for a member of Congress is provided in figure 4. I believe the scorecard should be a combination of general behaviors we expect of members of Congress coupled with specific objectives. The specific objectives can either be actions that we have asked the member to take, or it could be based on some list of top priority issues. Your individual scorecard for the members of Congress who represent you should reflect the way you want to measure your public servants. I advocate using a ten-point scale for each item you include on your scorecard for purposes of creating a standard yardstick. But you can use any scale you find helpful. Remember, the purpose of this scorecard is to support good voter behaviors by giving you an objective way to decide how to vote, to remember how and why you have voted in the past, and to communicate your opinions to others.

Engagement and Communication: Insisting on Transparency

One could say that the primary function of a member of Congress should be to understand and act on the will of the people whom she represents. To do this, each member of Congress must have an effective way to solicit and capture input from the people she represents. Constituents should provide specific input on specific issues on a regular basis. The notion that elected officials can or should intuit what the majority of Americans want from patterns of voting behavior seems inadequate.

We can be sure that our representatives and senators understand what we want them to do when each representative and senator clearly states that for which they feel accountable, along with the reason for this perceived accountability. As I have mentioned previously, a useful first step to achieving this level of transparency would be for all representatives and senators to take the political courage test sponsored by Project Vote Smart. In addition, each member of Congress should communicate back to the people the summary of the guidance they have received from the people. However, most members of Congress have not taken the political courage test. Furthermore, none of the congressional web sites I have surveyed include an anonymous, public summary of constituent correspondence.

An anonymous, public summary of constituent correspondence is important. I acknowledge that handling constituent correspondence can be more complex than one might think. But congressional staffs manage correspondence as one of their principal, routine functions. Each day, someone picks up and distributes the mail received at the Washington office. Electronic mail may also be distributed for review. All staff members may participate in the initial review of the mail since the subject may not be obvious until the letter or e-mail is opened. During this initial screening process, mail may be catalogued into a database that records the name of the constituent and the topic of the correspondence before being assigned to a specific staff member. Correspondence that seems to pertain to business matters is assigned to the staff person responsible for commerce, letters that seem to address military issues go to the staff person who handles military affairs, etc. The process is repeated at each of the member's offices that receive mail including those in her district or state. Responses are prepared and sent where appropriate. Correspondence that requires attention by senior staff or by the member herself is put into the appropriate queue. Eventually, staff members update the electronic record of the correspondence to show final disposition and any record of action associated with that correspondence.

The process of assigning a specific piece of correspondence to a general subject area in a database can be tricky. The categories that comprise such a database can mask or distort the actual subject or sentiment expressed in a letter or e-mail. Some categories for correspondence can include major pieces of legislation under current consideration, committees to which the member is assigned, and other general subjects (taxes, government spending, etc.) If a constituent tries to send an e-mail to a member, the system may require the constituent to pick a subject, and the subjects available may not include the precise subject about which the constituent is writing. I recently had this experience when I attempted to tell one of the senators from my state that I disapproved of his failure to take the Votesmart.org political courage test. There was no appropriate category for such a complaint about the senator's performance. I wrote a separate e-mail and letter about this issue, but it is likely that my correspondence will not be appropriately communicated to the senator. In cases such as this, we should be able to request changes to the categories available for classifying correspondence.

Members and senior staff should review summaries of constituent correspondence on a regular basis. This summary likely exists as a regular staff product in every congressional office—at least it should. This summary, with all information that could identify the sender removed, is what we should all insist on seeing on every member of Congress's web site. Even without the readily available commercial technology for accepting and displaying input online, preparing an anonymous summary for the web site would be a straightforward and logical extension of the function of managing constituent correspondence.

Without specific, transparent, two-way communication between voters and members of Congress, we are relying on faith and luck to determine whether our members of Congress are doing what they are being asked to do. Each of us is left looking at a list of priorities for some member of Congress without knowing how the member arrived at those priorities. We are left to assume that the priorities set forth by the member are priorities the member has been asked to address by other constituents, but we cannot know until we see the summary of constituent correspondence or some other way of capturing a current snapshot of voter sentiment.

Towards a Common Scorecard: Adding Basic Modern Technology to Member Websites

There may be a simpler way to put a scorecard in place that reflects the collective wisdom of the voters in a particular member's district or state in real time. A number of software solutions automate decision-market functionality—the ability to take weighted inputs from a population on a wide variety of topics in order to achieve a snapshot of the collective wisdom regarding the relative importance of the topics. Such functionality could easily be integrated into the web sites of each member of Congress.

The idea would be to allow voters registered in a district or state to create an account on the web sites of their members of Congress. Using these accounts, individuals could participate in decision markets on these, and only these, web sites. The decision market software would aggregate the input of all voters in accordance with some agreed-upon schedule, and would publish the list of voter priorities. These decision markets could rank the characteristics people within a district or state valued most highly in their elected public officials. Likewise, the decision markets could rank current issues in order of their importance to registered voters. People could write in issues of their own choosing and would not be constrained by a list or by the category system for correspondence developed by congressional staff.

A scorecard, like the sample shown in figure 4, could be dynamically created from the input of all voters registered in a district or state. The purpose of the first scorecard displayed at any given moment should be to reflect the relative importance of individual characteristics and issues as determined by the people registered to vote in a given district or state. Such a scorecard would aggregate the input of all registered voters. Since only voters registered in a particular member's district or state could participate in the decision market for that member's scorecard, voters could see at any time what their fellow citizens were telling the member of Congress to do.

It is important that the scorecard be used only to establish a priority of characteristics and issues and not for *publicly*[38] ranking the perceived performance of a member of Congress relative to characteristics and issues. Allowing use of this technology for public evaluation would risk undermining the independence of each voter's evaluation. The technology could increase the risk of creating information cascades liked those described earlier in this chapter. A better idea would be to allow individuals to print out the scorecard generated by the decision market technology and then privately rank their members' performance using their own best judgment.

The Ultimate Measure of Engagement: Voting

The most important outcome of engagement is to vote. Scorecards and performance management for elected officials are tools to help citizens quantify and measure the behaviors of those for whom they vote. We should not overvalue the tools relative to the purpose of the tools, which is to help us vote. The act of voting by a large, independent body of citizens is the best guarantee of our liberty. Our votes are the tools provided by the founding fathers to keep the republic more responsive to the will of the people than to the agendas of one or more special interests.

Without broad participation, our republic could drift into excessive partisanship to the point we have difficulty sustaining it. Washington explicitly warned us of the danger of partisanship when he wrote, "However combinations or associations... may now and then answer popular ends, they are likely, in the course of time and things, to become potent engines, by which cunning, ambitious, and unprincipled men will be enabled to subvert the power of the people and to usurp for themselves the reins of

---

38 Using the scorecard privately to create our own individual ranking of member performance is the point of the scorecard.

government, destroying afterwards the very engines which have lifted them to unjust dominion."[39]

The will of the people, if derived from an appropriately broad and balanced survey of the population, will provide a stable and wholesome azimuth for government action. This is the faith upon which our system of government rests. The law gives us the power to reshape our government through the ballot box every two years. We cannot condemn our government as ineffectual or wicked without at the same time condemning ourselves because our government is the product of the conscience, vision, and values we lend it as individual voters.

39 Washington's Farewell Address, http://avalon.law.yale.edu/18th_century/washing.asp

FIVE

The American Dream: Cooperation, Hope, Work, Luck

"I believe in the American dream. I believe my family has lived it over three generations, and I see others around me living it today. I believe cooperation, hope, hard work, and luck are all important aspects of the American dream."

—Stephen Tryon

America has long been known as a land of opportunity. I take that to mean that our country has a reputation for being a place where an individual can change their economic and social circumstances in a predictable way based on individual effort and merit. The American dream is the shorthand we use to capture the spirit of opportunity our country represents. Some today feel the American dream is slipping away. Many point to the widening economic gap between the very rich and the very poor as evidence that the American dream is dead. I want to propose that America remains a land of opportunity today, and that preserving the American dream is important for our long-term collective prosperity.

Being a land of opportunity, in the sense defined above, implies a comparison. In other words, when we say we are a land of opportunity, we have to provide additional context. For whom is the United States a land of opportunity? What is the nature of the opportunity we offer?

We might consider perspectives of both immigrants and native citizens in our exploration of whether America is still a land of opportunity.

Traditionally, America has been a land of opportunity for people leaving other countries where they have suffered oppression. The Statue of Liberty in New York Harbor is a potent symbol of opportunity for many people around the world. For these people, America offers an opportunity for a better life than they have known: more individual liberty, freedom from persecution, and the ability to provide a decent quality of life for themselves and their families. I have spoken with a number of immigrants over the past several years in a wide range of occupations. The people with whom I have spoken all seem happy with their lives in America, and say they are better off here than they were in their homelands.

Anecdotal evidence, of course, is not conclusive. There are undoubtedly many immigrants whose experience is not at all consistent with America as a land of opportunity. Others are victims of predatory practices by human traffickers and other criminals. I think these problems are not new, however. A cycle of persecution, victimization and suffering amongst immigrant populations is one of the ugly truths of American history. Yet we still find that, for much of the world, coming to America is a dream in itself.

In addition to the immigrant experience, we might reasonably expect a land of opportunity to afford accessible paths of economic and social mobility for those born here. Certainly, in the early days of our country, America's vast expanses of land, abundant natural resources, and laissez faire economics created significant opportunity for many. The landscape in the United States is different today. The face of opportunity in America may well have changed from this early model to a model emphasizing innovation within existing constraints. Our population has swelled, resources are not as accessible as they once were, and our economy is beset with complex regulations. But empirical evidence still indicates that America is a place where a Bill Gates or a Steve Jobs or a Howard Shultz can innovate their way to great opportunity and success.

The most powerful examples of opportunity in America are just such stories of people from humble beginnings creating great wealth by virtue of some Great Idea. Such stories are powerful because they testify to a *fair* system where innovators triumph based on merit. Many recent reports indicate the distribution of wealth in America has changed such that a larger share of wealth is concentrated in the hands of a smaller percentage of the richest Americans. It is appropriate for us to concern ourselves with these shifts because they raise the issue of systemic fairness. As long as we can address the fairness concerns with adequate numbers of success stories like those cited above, Americans will believe in the dream and will continue to practice the cooperative activities that support our individual liberty.

The roots of opportunity in America spring from a long tradition of individual liberty and consent-based governance. At the level of the individual citizen, this tradition engenders a sense of hope and empowerment that may be one of the greatest sources of our national power. But the individual liberty that provides the foundation for the American dream can be lost. Active engagement with our elected officials, especially in Congress, is important to preserving the American dream.

Political Power, Social Cooperation and Coercion

One way of comparing different kinds of government is by the level of coercion required to compel compliance with the government's authority. In societies where government needs little or no force to achieve compliance with the law by a majority of the population, we can say that a high level of social cooperation exists. The majority of people cooperate by complying with the law, and the government cooperates by ensuring laws do not oppress the people or constrain them unnecessarily. On this spectrum of social cooperation, the most autocratic dictatorships would be at one extreme and the most representative republics would be at the other. At both ends of the spectrum, governments may provide protection, order, and stable (if not fair) systems for resource allocation. The difference between governments at one end of the spectrum and those at the other is the level of coercion or force required to preserve order and stability.

While we may have a moral preference for the more highly cooperative end of the spectrum, I want to propose that it is not always possible for governments to *establish* order and stability without the use of force. The choice to cooperate within any system of government is an individual choice. Governments operate in societies made up of many individuals. Until some percentage of the population chooses to cooperate with a particular government, order and stability cannot emerge. Within any society, individual choices may coalesce around many different options for the structure and composition of the government. As these different factions compete for authority, force may be the only practical way to establish one coherent, supreme government. A government established in this way may be morally superior to the state of anarchy it replaces.

In the Declaration of Independence, Thomas Jefferson wrote that governments derive their just powers from the consent of the governed. Nearly two hundred years later, another revolutionary, Mao Zedong, wrote that political power comes from the barrel of a gun. I believe both statements are correct, but they refer to distinct regions on the spectrum of social cooperation. Furthermore, each statement reflects the experiences and environment that shaped Jefferson and Mao. The American conception of political power has been central to our image as a land of opportunity, but the evolution of political power in any society is inextricably related to the history of that society. We cannot simply prescribe what has worked here as the only or the best alternative for others.

Jefferson was born in 1743 into a relatively wealthy Virginia family. He inherited five thousand acres from his father and attended the College of William and Mary at age sixteen. Though he may be presumed to have been familiar with warfare because of his proximity to some of the fighting in the Seven Years War, he was sheltered from direct experience with this conflict. His perspective would have been that of a loyal British colonist observing a conflict between his country and the rival French monarchy. In all, he grew up in a stable society with adequate resources. As a young lawyer, he was elected to represent one of the counties of Virginia in the colonial legislature known as the House of Burgesses, and it was from this position that he emerged as a key philosophical leader of the American Revolution.

Mao, the son of a grain merchant, was born in 1893 in Hunan Province in central China. He grew up as the Qing dynasty was disintegrating around him; the country experiencing constant military conflict and frequent resource scarcity. The Boxer Rebellion (1898–1901) ended when a joint punitive expedition of eight foreign powers defeated Chinese military forces and imposed harsh fines. The last Chinese Empire disintegrated in rebellion in 1911. The abortive Republic of China failed in just a few years. China was governed by rival warlords and dominated by foreign influences for much of the period leading up to the Japanese invasion of Manchuria in 1937. From 1927 onward, Mao led military forces for the Communist Party in continuous warfare until his victory over Nationalist forces in 1949 led to the birth of the People's Republic of China.

Jefferson witnessed the colonists in America lose faith in a British government that insisted on imposing its will without the people's consent. He participated in the revolution whereby those people rejected the authority of the British government and established a representative government. The British government they rejected was a monarchy, but a monarchy with a relatively strong representative tradition compared to other contemporary monarchies. Over nearly six hundred years, from the Magna Carta onward, the English political tradition had limited the right of monarchs, increased protections for individual rights, and established a parliament. Colonial legislatures, such as Virginia's House of Burgesses, extended this tradition to North America. Military force was necessary to establish the American republic, but the war was only possible because of widespread support on the part of the people.

In the American Revolution, colonists, having lived in a somewhat cooperative society, resorted to collective violence when they felt the British monarchy was no longer adequately responding to their needs. Military power was a means to achieve the end of establishing a government that would better represent the will of the people in a cooperative society. Arguably, both the military power that made the revolution possible and the power of the government established by the revolution were products of the people's consent. The American army that fought the war was largely militia, and the new United States almost completely disbanded its standing army after the war.

Mao, on the other hand, witnessed an endless cycle of political power made real *only* through military force. In his youth, China was an environment where multiple competing parties continuously sought political dominance through military dominance. The political tradition of China at this time was more autocratic and less cooperative than that of the American colonies at the time of the American Revolution. Mechanisms to incubate mass social and political cooperation, like colonial Virginia's House of Burgesses, were not present. Even the establishment of the first Chinese Republic in 1912 was quickly subverted when Yuan Shikai, a former general and prime minister of the last Qing monarch, forced President Sun Yat Sen to give him supreme political authority.

The wars and uprisings that shaped Mao were not spontaneous uprisings based on mass consent—they were more like an incessant game of king of the hill, often arising from desperate scarcity caused by famine or flood. Mao himself participated in conflicts that initially seemed to continue in this vein, with various factions competing with each other and forming temporary alliances of convenience to gain political power or expel foreign invaders. Even the Chinese Civil War that gave birth to the People's Republic of China did not create a republic based on consent and social cooperation in the sense of the United States. Rather, Mao led a series of brutal purges to eliminate political and social rivals who might have continued the political and military turbulence that had plagued China since the collapse of the Qing Dynasty.

In light of their disparate experiences and social contexts, the different perspectives on political power expressed by Jefferson and Mao both seem accurate. Jefferson helped craft the Declaration of Independence fifteen months after the Battle of Lexington and Concord while the United States was embroiled in a revolutionary war that lasted eight years. In a sense then, one could say that the power of the United States government was a product of the barrels of the guns of the colonial militia and the nascent United States military. But in the United States it was possible to put aside the standing army after the American Revolution, whereas in China the People's Liberation Army has remained an essential guarantor of the political primacy of the People's Republic. So in the context of the United States, Jefferson was precisely correct. Military power was necessary to establish the American republic, but military power was neither necessary nor sufficient to sustain it. Mao needed military power not only to establish the People's Republic of China but also to sustain it.

The point I am making, that consent may be more or less necessary to legitimizing political power under various social conditions, is a point about practicality rather than morality. One may argue that consent is necessary for any government to have moral legitimacy. Alternatively, one could argue there is a moral basis for establishing a government that can provide basic collective security and stable resource allocation even when that government is not based on consent. I am making a much simpler point: a government may have to be established by force when there are no effective mechanisms of social cooperation through which to establish a government based on consent. In other words, there is a significant difference in the effectiveness of consent in legitimizing political power under different social circumstances.

I conclude that both Jefferson and Mao were correct. We band together in societies for the benefits of mutual protection, order, and stable systems for resource allocation. To the degree that a society has a strong notion of individual rights and the social mechanisms for protecting those rights, the consent of individuals is an important source of political legitimacy. In societies that do not have both a strong tradition of individual rights and the associated mechanisms for protecting those rights, political legitimacy becomes a function of the ability to protect and administrate—both of which can be guaranteed with military power. We can imagine the nations of the world along a spectrum of cooperation, based on the degree to which their populations engage in behaviors such as voting and paying taxes without coercion.

A Spectrum of Cooperation: Hope and Fear

We tend to think of the United States government as a thing apart from other types of government. We are democratic, and they are nondemocratic. We have freedom, and they do not have freedom. We elect our leaders while they are led by elites who sustain their grip on power through manipulations of the system. I think this view is dangerously wrong, and it leads us be complacent about the potential for abuses of power in our system. Despotism could never happen here, we think, because *we* are a republic.

The problem with this view is that it misses a key fact: the behaviors that characterize any society of any type are a function of the individual behaviors of the people who live in that society. Dictators can be benevolent—the problem is there is little chance of reliably sustaining benevolent leadership without the kinds of public mechanisms to control the leader that are usually absent in a dictatorship. There can be despotic abuses of power in our system, just as in other systems, if we are complacent and let them happen. The fact that there is a fire engine parked at the corner will not keep our house from burning down if no one turns on the water.

At the cooperative end of the spectrum, hope motivates people to comply voluntarily with laws and social norms in the expectation that compliance will, or can, lead to positive outcomes. Hope is the expectation of something good happening in the future. It is a powerful motivation for most people. It can help people overcome great adversity. Cooperative societies create reason for people to be hopeful. People can trust in a generally fair application of laws as well as in the security of their lives and property. Some of the most important cooperative behaviors are abiding by established laws, paying taxes, and voting. As more people engage in these behaviors, especially voting, the degree to which they identify with the policies and actions of the government increases. Under normal circumstances, on the cooperative side of the spectrum, positive behaviors and outcomes tend to create incentives for additional and more widespread cooperative behaviors.

At the coercive end of the spectrum, fear motivates people to comply with government directives. Fear works as a motivation as long as the government maintains a credible capacity to detect and punish noncompliance. Maintaining surveillance over an entire population is expensive. It tends to reduce government efficiency and increase mistrust within a population. In turn, government inefficiency and a lack of trust in society tend to decrease satisfaction. Less satisfaction with a government increases noncompliance with tax laws and other essential supports of government legitimacy, especially when people feel there is little risk of punishment for such behaviors. At the coercive end of the spectrum, negative incentives and outcomes tend to reinforce one another, making evolutionary improvement difficult.

Both hope and fear are emotions we experience as individuals. The satisfaction of a people with their government is a function of their individual quality of life, not of the words used to describe the form of their government. People may be quite happy with a government that is less representative than our government if, as individuals, they are able to pursue the dreams they consider important, they perceive the opportunity to improve their economic and social well-being, and they are proud of the actions the government takes on their behalf. Under such circumstances, telling a people that their government should give them more freedom is likely to have little effect. "More freedom" is an abstraction if current quality of life is satisfactory.

Unfortunately, the converse is also true: a people may not perceive a loss of freedom for a time if they are focused too much on short-term quality of life. This is particularly true if the perception of quality of life is shaped to an unprecedented degree by a special-interest-driven information stream. It is true regardless of whether the perception that is being shaped is that quality of life is getting better or that it is getting worse. In the 1992 election, one political advisor famously observed, "It's the economy, stupid." This was an effective way of capturing the essential truth that Americans will be satisfied with their government insofar as they are satisfied with their quality of life.

Quality of life is closely related to opportunity. The most tangible opportunity for most of us is economic opportunity, and that often comes down to whether or not we have a job or can get a job. But there are many ways to create jobs. A friend once told me a story about an American economist touring a work site where many people were excavating a trench with shovels. He asked if the manager had considered using machinery to speed up the project, and was told that shovels were better because they provided more jobs. He reportedly then asked if the manager had considered using teaspoons instead of shovels.

Some ways of providing jobs in the short term actually limit opportunity in the long term. Certainly there have been times in American history when we needed people to pick up shovels. But we have a political system that allows us to communicate to elected representatives that we are not content with shovels. We have a political system that allows us to hold those representatives accountable for creating better long-term opportunity than shovels provide. In the United States, the economic and social opportunity we call the American dream has been a downstream effect of individual liberty, the hope this liberty engenders in each of us, and the resultant level of cooperative behavior in our society.

Individual Liberty and the American Dream

On May 5, 2011, I had the privilege of addressing a joint commissioning ceremony in which the graduating ROTC cadets from the University of Utah and Westminster College took the oath of office and joined the army as "commissioned" officers. The president, in his role as commander-in-chief, issues commissions to military officers (and other officers in the executive branch) when they swear an oath to support and defend the Constitution of the United States against all enemies, foreign and domestic.

As I prepared my speech, I reflected on what my oath meant to me when I took it in 1983, and what it came to mean to me during my years of service. I settled quickly on the theme of my speech: the true power of the American military is not a tank or a ship or a plane. The true power of our military is the example of a young man or a young woman, properly led, serving in the United States Army, Navy, Air Force, or Marines. By the time these young men and women volunteers leave our shores to serve in foreign lands, they have been infected with an optimism that comes from growing up in a society where we consider it our right as individuals to build a better tomorrow for ourselves. They carry the power of this idea wherever they go, and they change those they touch by their example.

I believe the theme I chose for this speech reflects a deeper truth. The true power of America in every dimension—military, economic, diplomatic and informational—lies in the hope each American carries within us—the hope that we might realize our fullest potential based on our individual efforts and creativity. This is the American dream. It is our constitutional tradition that makes this dream possible.

We in the United States have nearly two hundred and forty years of tradition supporting collective decision-making processes based on our Constitution. With some major exceptions, such as our Civil War and the arduous struggle for civil rights for women and people of color, these processes have operated *mostly* by consent. The tradition of consent-based collective decision making that our Constitution made possible is the foundation of our individual liberty. And this liberty, balanced as necessary against the requirements of equal liberty for our fellow citizens, is the source of the hope that has made us one of the greatest nations on earth.

My Chinese friends are justifiably proud of the thousands of years of Chinese civilization. But we in the United States of America have a far longer tradition of consent-based collective decision making than any Chinese government in history. China was at war with itself and with foreign powers for most of the 20th century. One could argue that it was only from about the time of the Ping-Pong diplomacy of the early 1970s—just forty years ago—that China began its steady march up the spectrum of social cooperation to where it is today. The Chinese government is careful to place a priority on maintaining control as it reforms its markets, addresses widespread corruption, and increases individual liberties. Given China's relatively recent history of social turbulence and civil war, I don't see how its leaders could do otherwise.[40] The people of America should encourage and support China's progress while recognizing that American-style government is not necessarily the right solution for the people of China.

Individual liberty is central to the American paradigm: the classic rags-to-riches story of our country—the American dream—is a story of individuals prospering based on their wit and hard work. Our government contributed to this feature of our national character. I am open to the notion that government's contribution was simply to stay out of the way. I am also willing to allow for the view that our government's policies and practices have been a strong reason for the evolution of the American dream. In fact, the truth is probably somewhere in the middle. At the very least, here in the United States, government has presided over a society where individual

---

40 Note bene: the American Civil War broke out seventy-eight years after our Revolutionary War. The People's Republic of China will be sixty-four years old in 2013.

success stories could occur with sufficient frequency to create the hope that the American dream was within the grasp of each of us as individuals.

The reality of the American dream is important because it creates hope, and hope shapes individual behaviors that drive the cooperative character of our society. When we hope for some goal, and we believe that goal is within our reach, then we are more likely to invest time working to achieve the goal. There is significant evidence that this mechanism is self-fulfilling: hope motivates work, and work makes the hope a reality.

In his wonderful book, *Talent is Overrated*, Geoff Colvin makes a persuasive case that excellence in any endeavor is a function of hard work and deliberate practice.[41] Colvin examines cases of so-called prodigies, people widely believed to have been born with innate talent far beyond that possessed naturally by most others. Across every field of endeavor, whether in sports, art, science or business, he concludes that the difference in the level of achievement of those we consider "prodigies" is more a function of the time and deliberate practice they spend perfecting their skills than it is a result of any special natural gift.

If Colvin is right, and I believe he is, then the perception that the United States is a place where dreams come true may create conditions that, in fact, lead to a larger percentage of the population achieving their dreams here than elsewhere. In this case, the most important thing our society can do to support our pursuit of happiness is to preserve our ability to hope: to anticipate a positive return on the investments we make with constructive individual behaviors. We must preserve the perceived value of having a dream and investing in the behaviors that can make that dream a reality. One of the most basic of these cooperative behaviors is to vote.

A Case for the American Dream

At the Aspen Ideas Festival in July of 2012, I listened to Howard Shultz, the CEO of Starbucks, describe an initiative he was sponsoring to foster a dialogue on how to make America better. Mr. Schulz noted that he came from humble roots in New York City and felt an obligation to help others based on his own good fortune and success. Besides the marvelous initiative undertaken by Starbucks to make money available for small businesses in

---

41 Geoff Colvin, *Talent is Overrated* (New York: Penguin Group, 2008).

the United States, I was pleased to hear yet another story of a person who had a dream and found a way to achieve that dream here in the United States. I see evidence of the reality of the American dream all around every day.

As the executive with responsibility for human capital management—what I call the people systems—at Overstock.com, I have the privilege of seeing others realize parts of their dreams through their work. Systems such as our performance management, our online campus, and our tuition assistance provide tools for people to use in furthering their individual dreams within the company. The same tools may allow people to use their work at Overstock.com to further other life goals and dreams. This year, nearly 1,200 people have jobs at Overstock.com.

Consider the case of an employee I shall call Jim. Jim started work for Overstock.com in 2003, packing shipments for customers in the company's main warehouse. At the time, he was working for a company that provides temporary labor to help with seasonal surges in our shipping operations. Within a few weeks, Jim had an idea for improving the efficiency of the packing process. His supervisor allowed him to build a prototype, and the idea was a great success. Soon Jim was leading a team of packers.

I first met Jim when I took over direct responsibility for warehouse operations in August of 2005. He was a natural leader and was highly respected by people throughout the warehouse. As the holiday season approached, we added a night shift so we could keep up with the increasing volume of orders. The labor market was competitive, and we had some difficulty staffing the night shift. When I needed someone to take responsibility for the entire packing operation on the night shift, Jim volunteered. He did a terrific job. Early the following year, when we no longer needed the night shift, Jim took over responsibility for all packing operations in the warehouse.

I found out that Jim had a college degree, and was attending school at night working on an advanced degree in information systems. His dream was to ultimately have a career in technology or science. The company started a scholarship program as a first step toward the tuition reimbursement program we run today. Jim received one of the first scholarships in 2007, which helped him complete his studies. In 2008, Jim notified me he was graduating with a Master of Information Systems degree.

I told Jim I would try to get him a position in information technology as soon as I could spare him from logistics. It was another two years before I felt comfortable giving him up, but he continued to work diligently running our packing operation. In 2010, Jim moved to the technology department as a tester working on the software that powered warehouse operations.

Over the course of the seven years that we have known each other, Jim married his childhood sweetheart and started a family. A year or so ago, he sent me an email to tell me he was buying a house. And, back in 2005, with the help of a letter from Overstock.com confirming his great contributions to our team, Jim received his citizenship. Like my grandfather, Jim is an immigrant.

The story of Overstock.com, and how it came to be a successful company, is another American dream story. The CEO and founder, my friend Patrick Byrne, had an idea in the 1990s to use the Internet to sell a certain type of product. After being turned down by eighty-two of the private organizations that specialize in funding new business ideas, Patrick launched the company in October of 1999 with his own money and investments from family, friends and acquaintances. The story of Overstock.com is a book by itself, and that is a book I hope Patrick will write one day. My point here is simply to note that a special group of Americans invested a lot of their personal wealth to build a company that endures to this day as a part of the American economy. Over the past thirteen years, that company has provided great value for its customers, its partners and thousands of employees. The company's success is a dream fulfilled for my friend, and that success in turn has helped many others further their dreams.

The Threat to Individual Liberty

The American dream is real for each of us as long as we can hope to make our future better by virtue of our own effort and intelligence. The key to our ability to hope is our individual liberty. This liberty has been guaranteed by a representative government for over 236 years.

Our failure to adapt to the evolution of our information stream over the past forty years is a threat to our individual liberty because it has alienated us from our indispensable role as citizens in a representative government. The most important element in our role as citizens is our duty to vote with the full, independent, honest, and imperfect wisdom we can each bring to the ballot box. No matter what we have done (or not done) to prepare, we must all vote as best we can. The lesson of *The Wisdom of Crowds* is that we will make better choices together than we will when some of us choose not to vote. Voter participation data show a pronounced downward trend since 1972, and I believe a major cause for this trend has been our failure to adapt to the evolution of our information stream.

We are inundated with more information than we could possibly consume. Most of us don't have a strategy for confronting this tempest of information and are buffeted by the currents of the day. I do not believe these currents are centrally controlled as part of some nefarious conspiracy (yet), but they are governed by the economics of what sells and by our psychology as consumers. The content of the commercialized information stream, driven by economics and psychology, converges on some common themes. I call these themes the five myths. I believe the myths tend to distract us from our individual relationship with our members of Congress. I believe they lead us to more negative interpretations of events than is warranted by the facts alone.

The myths undermine our sense of hope, erode voter participation, and open a path for special interests to exert undue influence in Congress. Our perception of the rising power of special interests reinforces this negative trend. Political parties are special interests, and to the extent that our elected members of Congress vote to support a party position rather than to support the synthesis of their constituents' visions and values, they fail us.

When fewer of us vote, the gaps between our individual positions seem greater. Compromise is harder, and we drift toward partisanship and paralysis. When more of us vote, especially for our members of Congress, the opposite effect occurs. We empower our elected officials to find common ground.

Organizations and groups, including governments and political parties of all types, have no conscience unless they are comprised of people who insist that collective actions synthesize individual values appropriately. Conscience—the little voice in our heads that tells us whether or not we are acting in accordance with our values—is a function of individual consciousness, or self-awareness. Organizations, groups and governments build their collective "conscience" from the individual values of the people who participate in shaping the group's perception of itself.

When we choose to vote, we choose to participate in shaping a collective vision for America that reflects a synthesis of our individual values. This— and only this—is what lends America what we might call its collective conscience. When we fail to vote, we surrender the opportunity to participate in shaping our collective vision. In place of a synthesis of individual values, we are left with the lowest common denominator: political parties whose source of power is the sense of differentiation from other parties rather than a synthesis of the best of all parties. We are left with public servants who feel they must react to our fears rather than be a channel for our hopes. We are left with an America that is only as strong as its strongest special interest rather than the America that is, and always has been, greater than the sum of its parts.

Individual Liberty and Congress 2.0

As a preamble to this discussion, let me summarize the general case for which I have argued in this book:

(1) Americans have been passive consumers of information and government throughout our history.

(2) As long as the production of the commercial information stream was decentralized and the content of the stream was localized, this behavior allowed for adequate accountability for members of Congress.

(3) Over the past forty years, the production of the commercial information stream has become more centralized while the content of the stream has become less localized (geographically generic). This has made the information stream less relevant to our most important political relationship—our relationship to our members of Congress.

(4) We have not adapted to the change in our information environment.

(5) Passive consumerism of the modern information stream leads to unreflective, widespread acceptance of five myths that may be more false than true.

(6) These myths decrease faith in our government, suppress participation in federal elections, and contribute to a pernicious accountability gap in Congress.

(7) We can counteract the negative effects of the modern information environment by adopting the practice of accountability citizenship: being appropriately positive, appropriately informed, and appropriately engaged.

The first and most important step to accountability citizenship is for all of us to vote, to empower those around us to vote, and to hold our fellow citizens accountable for making the effort to vote. How others choose to vote is, of course, none of our concern. It is our right as Americans to have the choices we make on our ballot remain a secret. Whether our fellow citizens choose to vote, however, affects all of us. Surowiecki's *The Wisdom of Crowds* teaches us that the most extensive participation by individuals, independent of how others are voting, is likely to lead us to the best outcome. The ultimate measure of whether we are appropriately engaged, then, is whether we have voted ourselves and whether we have been a positive influence to encourage voting behavior by those around us.

The second most important step to accountability citizenship is to create an accountability relationship with our members of Congress based on transparency. We should require the use of modern technology to facilitate a dialogue between each member of Congress and their constituents. The technology exists to create functionality in the web site of every member of Congress that will create what I call Congress 2.0. This technology would allow individuals registered to vote in a particular member's district or state to record their top priority issues along with the rank they assign to each. Thus in real time, or at least in near real time, both member and constituents could see what people in the district considered the most important issues of the day, and how many people voted for any particular issue. Members of Congress should want to know this information, and they should want to share it with the people they serve. Leveraging collaborative technologies to create the right relationship and dialogue with our members of Congress is the key to being appropriately informed and engaged.

Establishing Congress 2.0 is critical to telling us the specific objectives for which we should hold members of Congress accountable. The essential aspect of our government—the thing we fought for in our revolution—is representation. We cannot know whether we are being properly represented unless we know that which the people have asked members to accomplish. Accountability citizenship is about people accepting their accountability to vote and participate, but it is also about our members of Congress accepting accountability for representing us.

The Constitution gives us the power to replace 87 percent of our Congress every two years. We should leverage this power by holding our members of Congress accountable for completing the specific, measurable, and achievable performance objectives that their constituents deem most important. We do not have to accept public servants who are more responsive to their party leaders than they are to the people they represent. When constituents ask for information on the positions and values of members of Congress, it is simply not acceptable for members of Congress to refuse to provide that information while citing direction given by party leaders.

The third most important step to accountability citizenship is to be appropriately positive in our posture towards the information that confronts us every day. Being appropriately positive means understanding our personal priorities and using those priorities to govern what we spend time watching, reading, and hearing. It also means using reason, as best as we can, to illuminate the perspectives and reasoning of those with whom we disagree. Finally, it means challenging the five myths wherever we find them by examining the evidence used to support them. Being appropriately positive requires us to become active rather than passive consumers of information.

Taken together, the three steps of being appropriately positive, appropriately informed, and appropriately engaged are the essential elements of accountability citizenship. Applying a positive structure of personal priorities and basic time management principles—being appropriately positive—inoculates us from the negative effects of information overload. Basic information processing skills and a rudimentary appreciation of our history and government enables us to be appropriately informed—to absorb important information from the free press while compensating for media bias. Together, being appropriately positive and appropriately informed empowers each of us to engage with our government in a way that restores and sustains an acceptable level of accountability, especially with our members of Congress. A systematic approach to individual citizenship, reinvented a bit for the information age, is all that is required to preserve the full power of the American dream for ourselves and for our children.

AFTERWORD

Thoughts in the Wake of the Recent Election

You cannot be an inactive spectator. We have too many high sounding words, and too few actions that correspond with them.

—Abigail Adams

This book began as a personal exercise in election-year therapy. I judge the process of writing the book a success. It has reminded me that the true power of America lies in the economic and social opportunity we call the American dream. We have the power to sustain that dream through powerful processes of consent-based decision making.

I am discouraged that voter turnout continues to be too low, and that only 18 percent of congressional candidates completed the political courage test sponsored by Project Vote Smart during the election of 2012.[42] In my view, the current level of transparency and political engagement between voters and their congressional delegations remains inadequate.

Like the Sarbanes-Oxley example cited at the beginning of this book, the recent drama surrounding the so-called fiscal cliff offers a useful example of what is possible when there is a specific objective to be achieved and a clear, public awareness of popular opinion regarding that objective. In the

---

42 http://votesmart.org/elections

wake of the election, we were told that our leaders were focused on averting a fiscal cliff set to kick in automatically after the first of the year. Expert consensus was that allowing these automatic measures to proceed without modification would send our country back into a recession.

Polls showed that a majority of Americans supported actions that would prevent any harm to the economy. President Obama and Congress exchanged proposals for various combinations of targeted tax increases and spending cuts. By early December, widely reported poll results showed that a strong majority of Americans favored increasing taxes on families making more than $250,000 per year.[43] Consensus on specific spending cuts was less clear.

Given the poll results and the high profile of the debate, Republican leaders in Congress felt they would be held accountable if they failed to reach a compromise. On January 2, Congress and the Administration passed compromise legislation that increased taxes for individuals making more than $400,000 and delayed many of the negative consequences of the fiscal cliff.[44] In my view, the widespread publicity about what the public wanted made the compromise possible. The lack of such a clear public consensus on spending cuts limited the extent of the compromise that was reached. In short, when Congress feels that the public is engaged, Congress acts in accordance with popular opinion.

I can think of no stronger argument for *Accountability Citizenship* and for the potential of our great nation. If we simply pick up the tools we have inherited, and put them to proper use, there are no problems we cannot solve and the best is still ahead for the United States of America. To preserve our liberty and realize the full potential of our republic, however, more of us must commit to being appropriately positive, appropriately informed, and appropriately engaged.

---

43 "Obama, Boehner Meet"; *Wall Street Journal*; December 10, 2012; p. A4.
44 "Deductons Limits"; *Wall Street Journal*; January 3, 2013; p. A6.

Appendix

Correspondence with Members of Congress

Bad men need nothing more to compass their ends, than that good men should look on and do nothing.

—John Stuart Mill

Voting is the most important measure of engagement. Other forms of engagement, however, are also important. Members of Congress have web sites funded by tax dollars. All of the web sites I surveyed offer quick ways for constituents to communicate electronically with the member. Web sites also have mailing addresses for the member. This contact information is also available for every member of Congress at VoteSmart.org.

In this appendix, I provide samples of three letters I referenced earlier in this book. Some of these sample letters are based on letters I actually sent to my congressional delegation last year. The first encourages the members to take the Political Courage Test sponsored by VoteSmart.org (not a single one of the members of Congress representing me had taken this test as of the date of this publication). The second letter requests that decision-market technology be added to the member's web site to improve transparency. The third letter requests that members adopt certain behaviors I might reasonably associate with balancing the budget (if all members were to adopt these behaviors).

Once you have taken the time to craft letters for whatever issues you deem most important for our country, you can easily cut and paste the text into an e-mail. I encourage you to use every means of communication possible to convey your vision and values to your congressional delegation. You should pay attention to any responses you receive from your congressional representatives; the timing and substance of the response will give you some indication of the procedures in place for handling constituent correspondence.

Establishing accountability with our congressional delegation requires two-way communication. We have to communicate to our representative and senators what we would like them to do. They have to communicate back to us what they have been asked to do in aggregate, by all voters in their district or state. Then they have to communicate back to us what they achieved relative to that for which the voters asked. I hope the sample letters in this appendix make it easier for people to begin this process of communication with the members of their congressional delegations if they are not already engaged in such communication.

Your name
Your street address
Your city, state and zip code
Date

Senator _____**
_____ Senate Office Bldg.**
Washington, D.C., 20510

Dear Senator _____,

I am a registered voter in your state. I am writing to request that you complete the 2012 Political Courage Test sponsored by Votesmart.org.

Currently, the Project Vote Smart web site has the following message about you displayed on their site:

"_____ refused to tell citizens where he stands on any of the issues addressed in the 2012 Political Courage Test, despite repeated requests from Vote Smart, national media, and prominent political leaders."

I find it unacceptable that you have not responded to this nonpartisan citizen organization that exists to facilitate our democratic process.

If there is a good reason why you have refused to take this test, please illuminate me. I can think of no reason why a public servant in your position would shy away from a clear statement such as the Political Courage Test.

I look forward to hearing from you.

Sincerely,
Your name

**Names and addresses for your Representative and Senators may be found at VoteSmart.org.

Your name
Your street address
Your city, state and zip code
Date

Senator _____**
_____ Senate Office Bldg.**
Washington, D.C. 20510

Dear Senator _____,

I am a registered voter in District __. I am writing to request that you modify your web site to include decision-market technology that will allow us to see, in near real-time, what our fellow registered voters are saying about the issues they consider priorities.

Currently, voters have no way of knowing what other voters are requesting from their members of Congress. Yet technology exists, today, to insert a restricted access application into your web site that would allow voters registered in your district to record their opinions on the subjects that are most important to them as well as their specific views on these subjects. That same technology would allow you to better discharge your duties as our Representative by seeing what the people want from you. You could easily share a summary snapshot of issues, with the numbers of people for and against, on your web site. This proposal is essential for transparent government in the information age.

The limitations of the current system for handling constituent correspondence are many. The most serious, in my view, is that you currently cannot distinguish registered voters in your district from those outside your district. My proposal would solve that issue.

In the interim, I request you provide a summary of the correspondence you have received year to date broken down by topic, number of pieces of correspondence, and pro /con. A simple pie chart will suffice, and could be easily displayed on your web site. This information is probably nothing more than the summary I assume you are receiving periodically from your staff. For example, one piece of the pie chart might be Affordable Care Act (Con) with a number in it. Another piece might be Affordable Care Act (Pro) with a number in it. I suspect that the largest piece of the pie chart will be labeled "Other," This is perhaps the major drawback of your current system that decision-market technology could alleviate. Please provide me a summary of the constituent correspondence you have received year to date, and your thoughts on the proposal to incorporate decision-market technology into your web site.

Sincerely,
Your name

**Names and addresses for your Representative and Senators may be found at VoteSmart.org.

Your name
Your street address
Your city, state and zip code
Date

Senator _____**
_____ Senate Office Bldg.**
Washington, D.C. 20510

Dear Senator _____,

I am a registered voter in District __. I am writing to request that you adopt the following behaviors I feel are essential to balancing the budget:

(1) do not vote for any budget that calls for more spending in a given year than the government expects to take in;

(2) do not vote for any legislation to which measures have been added to authorize or appropriate funding for non-related activities or projects (earmarks); and

(3) report the budgetary effect of all legislation using the 3 reference points of current spending, Congressional Budget Office baseline and Office of Management and Budget baseline.

If every Member of Congress were to follow these behaviors, I believe we would be able to balance the budget quickly.

I believe balancing the budget has to be treated as a national priority on the same order as any other initiative for which we feel we need to spend money. Certainly, the failure to achieve some fiscal discipline will put at risk all of the good that might be accomplished through the other measures for which we might authorize and appropriate funds. I look forward to hearing your thoughts on this important issue.

Sincerely,
Your name

**Names and addresses for your Representative and Senators may be found at VoteSmart.org.

Index